**DAY BOOK**

THE PINE TREE BOOK

Here is a colorful, complete and accurate guide to the most familiar but most confusing of American evergreens, the widespread, useful and romantic pine tree. Pines grow worldwide in the Northern Hemisphere and many species have been introduced to North America from their native habitats, so that to identify any given tree one must be able to recognize kinds of trees that originated elsewhere. Thus this is actually a worldwide guide. The most important species are illustrated in full color—32 in all—and give a general description, range, usefulness and include an identification key covering needles, cones, branches, and bark. Various species of birds and animals are included in the illustrations where they are closely tied to a particular pine, and in over 60 line drawings the general shape of both familiar and rare species are shown. There is a complete glossary and a full index. This is a splendid addition to any nature library.

THE
PINE TREE
BOOK

Based on the Arthur Ross Pinetum in Central Park

by

RUSSELL PETERSON

Illustrations by
PATRICIA WYNNE

With a foreword by Henry Hope Reed

THE BRANDYWINE PRESS, INC
NEW YORK

This book was edited and produced by
The Brandywine Press, New York
Clarkson N. Potter, President

Design and Production by Helga Maass

Library of Congress Catalogue Number: 79-65977

ISBN: Cloth 0-89616-005-X
     Paper 0-89616-006-8

First Edition

Acknowledgement

I should like to thank Henry Hope Reed and Frederick McGourty
of the Brooklyn Botanic Garden for their help with the manu-
script; Helga Maass, for her work in designing this book; Diana
Haring, for her able assistance in research; and, in particular,
Patricia Wynne, for her tireless pursuit of accuracy in her splendid
illustrations.

The Author

Contents

Various species in Central Park nursery, *Photograph by Carl Mydans*

Preface

It is with much pleasure and I dare say with a sigh of relief that I note the final bringing together for publication of this definitive volume on the pine tree. It is based on the Pinetum that I established in Central Park in 1971 and which is now largely completed.

My objective was originally somewhat limited, having to do with improving the appearance of the northern end of the Great Lawn. There were unsightly buildings, an unattractive playground and other such objects in this bare and desolate area that would be well screened with a liberal planting of American White Pines. The white pine is excellent for screening and provides needed color and shows to a special advantage during those long winter months when the deciduous trees are bare and nature's hardness is all about us. We soon realized that by adding a variety of specimens we would find out what other types of pine trees would also flourish in Central Park. An educational purpose would also be served by making readily accessible to the public a wide variety of different types of pines for comparative study.

I am much indebted to Mr. Henry Hope Reed, who wrote the introduction to this book, for his counsel and advice throughout the establishment of the Pinetum. My indebtedness is also to Mr. Russell Peterson, the distinguished naturalist, who has provided us with an authoritative and at the same time an interesting narrative; to Patricia Wynne for the 32 authoritative color plates which add much attraction and usefulness to the text; and to Mr. Clarkson Potter, publisher of the Brandywine Press, for his enthusiasm and interest in the project. Special acknowledgment is also due to the Central Park Community Fund for its cooperation.

I would like to close my remarks with a quotation from Bailey's *Standard Cyclopedia of Horticulture:*

"What the apple is among the fruits, what the oak is among the broadleaved trees of the temperate zone, the pines represent among the conifirs, excelling all other genera in this most important family in number of species, in fields of distribution, in extent of area occupied, in usefulness and importance to the human race. No other trees of the temperate zone have contributed so much to the building up of civilization, and no other, it may be predicted, will continue longer to fill the important place in the household of civilized men . . .''

Arthur Ross
New York City, June, 1979

Foreword

The most important *visual* change in Central Park in recent years has been the Arthur Ross Pinetum. Yet this stretch of green has gone unnoticed although it stands just northwest of the Metropolitan Museum of Art, directly north of the Great Lawn—unnoticed because, instinctively, when it comes to physical change in the city, we think in terms of steel, brick, glass and concrete rather than of trees and shrubs.

The site was hardly worth noticing prior to the coming of the pines, its most conspicuous feature consisting of two back walls, one of the Maintenance Building and the other of the Central Park Police Precinct. An abandoned children's wading area occupied the corner near the Maintenance Building, and a more than customary shabbiness set the tone of the area. The general condition and the rear walls could not very well escape the attention of Mr. Arthur Ross, a born-and-bred New Yorker who, for a number of years, had made a habit of walking around the Great Lawn. In 1971, he approached Cornelius M. O'Shea, Park Department horticulturist, to explore what could be done with the area. As it turned out, O'Shea and the author of this preface, as Curator of Central Park, had wanted to bring back evergreens that, at one time, had been a distinction of the park. So why not begin near the Maintenance Building?

Arthur Ross and Mr. O'Shea then decided to plant 35 White Pines. But this would never have been possible without the permission and encouragement of Commissioner August Heckscher. As the trees did well, Arthur Ross outlined a project of turning the grove into a pinetum. This has since been accomplished with the approval of subsequent Park Commissioners namely, Messrs. Richard Clurman, Edward Weisl, Jr., Martin Lang and Gordon Davis. What had been no more than a modest equivalent of a New England pine lot has been transformed into the Arthur Ross Pinetum, which, at the time of publication, numbered 600 trees.

The site of the Pinetum, it should be explained, was not part of the original park. Most of it was covered by the Old

Receiving Reservoir opened in 1845, more than a decade before Frederick Law Olmsted and Calvert Vaux produced their Greensward Plan (1858) for the park. (The present reservoir, the New Receiving Reservoir, goes back to 1863.) The Old Reservoir was not surrendered until 1929, at which time it was emptied. In the first years after the Panic of 1929, impoverished squatters invaded the area and found shelter in shanties. Then it was filled again, landscaped and opened to the public in 1936, with the Great Lawn as its chief ornament.

The Old Reservoir had concealed the Maintenance Building and the Precinct Station but with its removal the walls of the two buildings became visible. The landscaping of 1936 did little to hide them, something Olmsted and Vaux would never have tolerated. This the Pinetum has finally accomplished.

Other than creating a green tapestry to screen two buildings, which, although essential, had nothing to do with the park landscape, the Pinetum has made possible the return of pine species once plentiful in the park, especially along the West Drive. At one time the sweep of evergreens there was so extensive that it was known as the Winter Drive, but today the Winter Drive no longer exists. In fact, until the coming of the Pinetum, only the Austrian Pine, *Pinus nigra,* with an occasional White Pine and Japanese Black Pine, was to be seen in the park. Here, then, was an opportunity to test many species for possible park use.

No pines stood within the park boundaries when the site was chosen for park use. And it was not until 1858, with the implementation of the Olmsted-Vaux plan, that pines were first planted. By 1873, according to the official plant list, there were the following: Austrian Pine *(P. nigra),* Corsican Pine *(P. nigra,* var. *poiretiana),* Swiss Mountain Pine *(P. mugo),* Red or Norway Pine *(P. resinosa),* Scotch Pine *(P. sylvestris),* Jeffrey Pine *(P. jeffreyi),* Ponderosa Pine *(P. ponderosa),* Pitch Pine *(P. rigida),* Balkan or Macedonian Pine *(P. peuce),* White Pine *(P. strobus),* Dwarf White Pine *(P. strobus,* var. *nana).*

A decade or so later Professor Charles Sprague Sargent, director of Boston's Arnold Arboretum and certainly the outstanding dendrologist or student of trees of the day, visited the park, During his visit he noted that the White Pine thrived well in the park but the rest, including the Austrian Pine, were suffering.

Another list, this one published in 1903, offers these: Austrian Pine *(P. nigra),* Himalayan Pine *(P. wallichiana),*

Corsican Pine (*P. nigra,* var. *poiretiana*), Swiss Mountain Pine *(P. mugo),* Scotch Pine *(P. sylvestris),* Swiss Stone Pine *(P. cembra),* Ponderosa Pine *(P. ponderosa),* White Pine *(P. strobus),* Shortleaf Pine *(P. echinata).* Quite obviously the Forestry Section of the Park Department had replaced the dead and dying trees that had caught the attention of Professor Sargent.

Around the time of World War I, a change took place in park policy. For some reason, when pines died, they were replaced by broadleaved deciduous trees. For more than fifty years, from about 1910 to 1965, no pines except the Austrian Pine were planted. In the late 1960s, horticulturist O'Shea began to plant a few White and Himalayan Pines on the east side of the park. Today, the Arthur Ross Pinetum has dramatically made up for the one-time neglect.

The Pinetum, as can be seen from the map on the end papers, has been divided into sections. In one there are predominantly White Pine, in another Himalayan. At the western end, varieties, such as the Weeping White Pine, have been collected. At the eastern end, Richard Webbel, of the well-known landscape firm of Innocenti & Webbel, selected and planted a mixture of Korean, Austrian, Japanese White and the native White Pine.

Yet another facet of the Pinetum is the nursery just south of its western end. It is part of a project organized by Arthur Ross and Dr. David F. Karnofsky, Forest Geneticist of the Cary Arboretum, a division of the New York Botanical Garden. Dr. Karnofsky grows young pines in the nursery where they get special attention. In addition, root stock grown in the Cary Arboretum greenhouse in Millbrook, Dutchess County will be grafted—at the proper time—with scions taken from pines in the Pinetum. The result will be trees that can be grown safely in an urban setting.

A similar program is being carried out with seeds collected in the Pinetum. The seeds are taken to the Cary Arboretum where they are stratified. Although the word "stratify" stems from the practice of putting seeds between layers or strata for safekeeping, it now is used to mean the process of aiding germination of dormant seeds by variations in temperature. For example, cold stratification, which most pine seeds must undergo, calls for keeping pine seeds at a temperature of 40 degrees Fahrenheit for two months. Germination follows. One result of stratification, of course, is that they all germinate at the same time, which makes possible a quantity of seedlings of the same age.

Seedlings from all parts of the world are planted in the nursery and later moved to the Pinetum and elsewhere in the park, depending on how they support local conditions. It is expected that some species selected will be planted here for the first time in the United States. The Arthur Ross Pinetum, quite obviously, has come a long way from the clump of White Pines, which O'Shea planted in 1971.

In making possible the Pinetum, Arthur Ross was well within a horticultural tradition, to be sure, of recent origin. The first mention of the word, pinetum, is to be found in James Forbes' *Pinetum Woburnense* published in London in 1834. He made use of it in a much larger sense than that given it today or, for that matter, as adopted in Central Park, namely accepting it as synonymous with evergreens. The pinetum at Woburn, one of the best known places in England as the home of the Dukes of Bedford, was actually begun in 1743, by the Third Duke as a plantation of "evergreens."

In England, interest in pines, as apart from other evergreens, occurred earlier. One notable example was the planting of our native White Pine in 1705, by the Duchess of Beaufort at Badminton and by the First Viscount Weymouth at Longleat. So noted was this last plantation that the noble lord left his name to the tree, at least in Europe where the White Pine is known as the Weymouth Pine. With the coming of the picturesque or "natural landscape," the *jardin à l'anglaise,* the vogue of tree and shrub collecting caught on, usually in the form of arboretums that would, of course, include a section of evergreens.

The first pinetum in the old sense of solely evergreens is generally accepted as having originated with Lord Grenville at Dropmore near Windsor, occurring around 1810. A generation later several others were in existence, the one at Woburn being the best known. What proved to be the incentive was the importation into England of species from our Pacific Coast. In the 1820s, an extraordinary Scotsman, David Douglas, was sent there by the Royal Horticultural Society to gather all kinds of plants and seeds. The indefatigable Douglas, for whom the Douglas Fir is named, discovered seven of the seventeen known pine species of the West Coast. Among those he found and named were the Ponderosa Pine and the Sugar Pine, in 1826.

Only shortly before, another plant collector, the Dane, David Wallich, had sent back seeds of the Himalayan Pine *(P. wallichiana)* from India. He and Douglas were just two of the hundreds of plant seekers exploring the world for all kinds of material, which was sent back to Western Europe. Much of it then came to this country, chiefly via England.

If England was at the forefront in importing pine species, France was leading in investigating the use of the pine. This may well have been due to the tree being grown in quantity for timber and for stabilizing soil. Probably the largest single stretch of landscape transformed by the pine is that of the former sand dunes to the south and west of Bordeaux in the country called the Landes. Here in 1787-1788, Nicholas-Thomas Brémontier planted the Cluster, or Maritime Pine *(P. pinaster)*, to halt the march of sand dunes invading a prosperous agricultural country.

In this country the interest in collecting plants proved somewhat slower. However, John Bartram, the great American collector of the eighteenth century, had a botanical garden on the banks of the Schuykill as early as 1730. The second such garden was that of Humphrey Marshall in Chester County outside of Philadelphia in 1773. A third, south of the town of West Chester, also in Pennsylvania, was founded in 1800, by the Peirce brothers. It is now part of the magnificent Longwood Gardens built by the late Pierre S. du Pont. The giant trees on the place date back to the Peirces.

These were modest plantations compared to those in England and to those that came later in this country. The concept of the true arboretum did not take hold in America until after the middle of the last century. In 1852, Horatio Hollis Hunnewell began one on his estate at Wellesley overlooking Lake Waban, across from the Wellesley College Campus. (It is one open to the public, to be visited by permission.)

Another was that of Henry Winthrop Sargent at "Wodenethe" near Beacon, New York, who is immortalized by the *Tsuga canadensis,* var. *pendula,* or Sargent's Weeping Hemlock. A third was that of Josiah Hoopes, a nurseryman at West Chester, not far from Longwood Gardens. Yet a fourth, well known in its time, was that of Charles Anderson Dana, publisher and editor of the New York *Sun.* In 1872, he began his pinetum as part of an arboretum on Dosoris Island at Glen Cove on Long Island.

About this time there began the shift from the private to the semi-public and public sector in creating arboretums. In 1872, the same year Dana began his, Charles Sprague Sargent established the Arnold Arboretum on parkland owned by the city of Boston. The first cousin of Henry Winthrop Sargent, he soon made it the most famous of American plant collections. Its collection of pine species alone numbers thirty-three. The New York Botanical Garden in the Bronx came later, in 1891 to be exact. It has 25 species and 37 varieties in its pinetum, with 31 species and 48 varieties throughout the Garden. The Brooklyn Botanic Garden, started in 1909, counts seventeen species.

Across the nation the collecting of pines is now standard policy in the creating of arboretums. One of the more interesting is the Institute of Forest Genetics of the United States Forestry Service in Placerville, California. Begun as a private venture in 1925, by James E. Eddy, it now specializes in hybridization.

As for pinetums being part of public park systems, the examples are few. One of them, where the pine groves are conspicuous in their variety and quality, is that of Monroe County, New York, which includes the parks of the City of Rochester.

The Arthur Ross Pinetum is thus part of a continuing tradition going back several centuries. Where it is different, other than being in the nation's most famous park, is that it joins the traditional aspect to the latest scientific techniques, with the Park Department and the Cary Arboretum cooperating to develop pines for the metropolitan area. Its future development will be well worth following.

. . . .Henry Hope Reed

Swiss Mountain Pine in Central Park,
Photograph by Carl Mydans

Introduction

A pine tree is a cone-bearing plant of a woody, aromatic nature that is commonly found in forms that are pleasing to the eye, to the palate (for many pine seeds are both succulent and nutritious), and of importance in the entire life span of Boreal Man.

All of which is true, but such an introductory sentence might be written about a hundred other plants or animals, or minerals. And there can be, and are, countless books written about any subject on-or-off the Earth: on plumbing, nuclear fission, Ming Dynasty porcelain, whales, or of mites that inhabit the ears of baboons. And there are always people to read them—albeit in vastly divergent numbers dependent upon the subject.

There are many books on pines. There are many good books on pines. This is because pines are a much-loved entity.

I used the term ''Boreal Man'' when I could just as well, and more easily, have said Northern, not as an exercise in pomposity but because Boreas was the Greek god of the north wind. Pines are ''of-the-north.'' *There are no pines below the equator.* That is, until man first carried them there in the 1800s there were not. Or, excluding a scant few acres of the island of Java, then one can safely and accurately say that pines are truly a northern tree. There are austral trees by the score that *look* like pines and *seem* to be pines, but they are *not* pines. And so Boreas was indeed rightly and properly brought into it.

Further, Boreas (so it is related in Greek mythology) had a mistress, a nymph named Pitys. And Pitys' gentle duty was to care for and attend to all pine trees in the godly realm. She must indeed have been tender and lissome and sweet—and old Boreas was scarcely any bargain, what with all that puffing and blowing (as any antique map will show you); but she strayed near Pan with his laughter and his flute and his winning ways.

Boreas found out about her flirtation and was so enraged that he threw her against a rocky ledge where she herself was turned into a pine tree. The limpid resin drops one

15

sees on the torn limbs of a pine tree, broken by the fierce North wind, are most obviously the tears of poor Pitys lamenting her loss of the fun-loving, irresponsible, irrepressible Pan. At any rate, they are quite genuine tears as anyone can see—else how could it be possible that so staid a personage as a modern taxonomist should choose to name *Pinus pityusa* in commemoration of her, a lonely pine that grows on the rocky slopes facing the sea along the borders of the Black Sea. *Pinus* is the Latin. The Greek for "Pine" is *Pitys*.

And so, pines are a tree of the north. They are born from a seed dropped from a symmetrical case called a "cone." As we shall see, there are many other coniferous (cone-bearing) trees, e.g., firs, larches, spruces, etc.; but pines are, of them all, the most useful, the most esteemed, and the most beautiful.

A pine seed consists of a hard shell wrapped in a leathery, membranous coating, inside which is cradled the kernel that is scientifically labeled the *endosperm*. The seed is generally borne to the ground by a single wing that is capable of carrying the seed well beyond the limits of distribution if left to falling without assistance. The foraging of birds and animals also helps to carry the seeds to new ground.

Within the kernel is the embryo pine, no more or less miraculous a spark of life than a bean in its awakening and growth. But what makes one spread into a bush and another ascend to the looming height of over two hundred feet? Of course the answer is in its genetic make-up, more "programmed" to exactitude and accurate replication than the most advanced of man-made circuitry. Sugars, amino acids, nitrogen, lipase, glycerin and other agents are all tightly packed into the tiny embryo. Once triggered, the sun at once feeds it, warms it and draws it upward. The root descends in search of nutrients and the entire framework of root, stem and embryonic leaves (cotyledons) virtually trembles with life and vigor, and growth advances at a rapid rate.

As the young tree matures, the vertical growth is determined by the "terminal shoot," the topmost bud that develops into the trunk of the tree from which branches will emerge. Branches tend to grow horizontally because the hormonal content of the terminal leader retards their vertical growth.

At first the tiny tree is composed of nearly pure cellulose. But from twelve to fourteen days following germination a substance called *lignin* combines with cellulose within the cells of the young plant and bonds to form a hardened tissue called "wood." The process is repeated and more and more height and girth are achieved by the plant until it changes from a virtual grass-blade form into a "tree."

What one first sees in the distance is the *form* of a pine tree. It is "shaped" like a pine. But that is in comparison to trees other than pines.

When pines of one species are seen together, of course, all individuals within that species will have variations of form and structure. But they will all more or less fit into an obviously identical group. Even should there be three different *kinds* of pines, and all with different shapes, identification would seem to be no more difficult. Not so, however. Both age and conditions of the habitat in which the pine grows cause the norm of external appearance to alter, often in a drastic way. For instance, in considering a five-year-old Scotch Pine, a twenty-year-old Dwarf Swiss Mountain (Mugo) Pine, and a sixty-year-old Swiss Stone Pine: the Scotch Pine can be small and stunted rather than tall; the Mugo Pine—an acknowledged dwarf—grows to a height of forty feet under some conditions; and the Swiss Stone Pine—in age—can look like an entirely different tree one-half that age.

Next, there are the needles: the Swiss Stone Pine has five to a sheath (the basal filamentous coating, which attaches the set of needles to the branch); the Scotch Pine has but a uniform two to a sheath; but we soon find out that the Mugo Pine *also* has two to a sheath.

Next, come the cones, then the branches, and then the bark. In each, one can see similarities and dissimilarities. The answer lies in keys to the illustrations and in the necessary cross-checking. Physical form helps. But it is the total identity—as in the whole person—that isolates the true character of the individual tree.

First, one sees the tree. It is a pine tree. Second, its needles are green; we reach up and see what they are like. Third, the cones on the ground are simply husks, like discarded eggshells; we reach to a branch and examine a fresh cone. Fourth, in so doing, we feel the branch itself. Fifth, the trunk with its bark is nearby; we scrutinize its character.

Other than those things, the flower buds are seasonal, the inner chemistry and genetic structure is sealed from us as though in a vault, its roots are buried underground, and the tree's paleobotanical history and taxonomic placement awaits our finding the simple *identity* of the tree.

NEEDLES

It is said that, "All healthy pines have green foliage." But, of course, "green" is a mixture of yellow and blue—and pines are indeed green, but certainly they vary in the matter of hues and shades. However, variation in greens is just that; yellows or browns indicate an unhealthy tree. The green coloring is a direct result of chlorophyll content.

Pine needles, having matured from the soft, primary cotyledons of its early stages, grow in bundles contained within a sheath that develops and protrudes from an embryonic core within the branch. The number of needles in a sheath varies from one to eight, but the majority of species commonly have from two or three to five to a sheath. Only two species, for instance, of four-to-a-sheath needles are known to exist, and only one with six to seven to eight.

It has been accurately stated (Mirov and Hasbrouck) that, "Each pine needle is the uppermost terminus of a strand of water coming without interruption from the tree roots, perhaps two hundred feet below." This water is channeled through vascular conduits ending within each needle in either single or double bundles from which stomata (mouthlike openings, capable of opening and closing) extrude to the waxy surface to admit air to the interior or to expel waste gases and surplus water.

The pictured cross-sections show how pine needles of varied bundle-content are divided and how their vascular channels, stoma openings, and resin canals are situated within each needle. Also, an example is shown of needle length, a characteristic that seems to vary with climate and altitude, e.g., the shorter the needle the more harsh its environmental niche.

In closely examining the needles, for comparative analysis, our attention should be given to the following:

1. The number of needles to a sheath.

2. Shades and hues of green, which vary considerably.

3. The character of the needles, which may be: slender or stocky; stiff or flexible; long or short; bent, straight or twisted (or, distressingly, sometimes all three); single or in clumps; their margins either marginal or medial; stomata either on one or both surfaces; and the basal sheath either short or long.

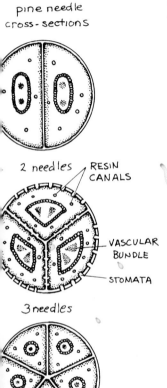

pine needle cross-sections

2 needles

RESIN CANALS

VASCULAR BUNDLE

STOMATA

3 needles

5 needles

18

4. And, although all species are deciduous, they vary in the number of years in which each eventually falls, (Since the trees can retain their leaves in winter, they are commonly called "evergreen" trees.)

While meaning little by itself, all of this information about needles *compared* to that from other species of pine will give a substantial base from which to start. The complexity of the subject seldom produces an instantaneous revelation, even with textbook in hand, for other species often present the same lengthy list of similarities. It is the *dissimilarity* then, finally, which will prove to be our last piece of the puzzle.

CONES

The pine cone is an extraordinary instrument. Most, at any rate, are symmetrical and formed into ordered rows of protective scales—actually small doors with a sharp lock on each latch. But the cone is only the carrying-case, as in a jeweler's box—however ornate; once the diamond ring (the seed) is removed, the box is useful only for pins and paper clips. And to continue the analogy, the ring is only the kernel (a supportive setting). Ultimately, it is the tender ivory-colored rod of the embryo pine that reveals itself to be our "diamond."

Even though our cones are just carrying-cases soon to be husks, in the matter of comparisons, they are another of our substantial aids to identification.

We shall then look to the cones to be:

1. Solitary or in clusters.

2. Directly attached to the branch, or with an obvious stalk attachment.

3. Round, cylindrical or ovoid.

4. Forward pointing, erect or pendulous.

5. Long and straight; long and curved; short and fat; symmetrical or off-center.

6. *Size:* longer than wide, or wider than long.

7. *Color:* browns, greys, yellows, oranges, tans, ochres, reddish-browns, reddish-yellows, greens, etc.—all, depending not only upon age but upon the light in which they are seen.

typical pine cone

8. *Scales* (of the cones): short and wide, or wider than short, or longer than wide; keeled; with or without a ''prickle'' (a sharply-hooked or at least pointed projection on the outside of the scales).

9. *Seeds:* round, oval or irregular; uniform in coloration or mottled; wings long or short, etc.

BRANCHES

Shrubs are woody plants that have no central trunk but are all ''branches,'' in effect. Pines have a trunk—the after-product of the vertically ascending leader with its whorls of new growth. Branches are also an after-product—like the lower tiers of skyrocket bursts that fall away symmetrically from the brilliant ascension of each successive explosion from the velvety canopy above.

First, it must be ascertained whether branches are young or old. If young, they are often revealing as to color: ranging from light browns to greens, to purples, to darker browns and greys. Also, they are either smooth or roughened; pubescent, hairy, scaly or checkered.

Their direction of growth (either upward, horizontal, or downwards) is often of interest but rather less supportable in the matter of scientific identification.

BARK

Bark, also, like the direction of the branches, is subject to great variation; age being, perhaps, the most obvious cause of it. Still, bark is often of great help in identifying a species. The ''bark'' we see and touch is actually only the outer, dead tissues—a crust—of the still living and growing ''inner bark.''

Bark may be: thickly or thinly crenulated; with very thick irregular plates or without plates at all; smooth . . . an actual description is as follows: ''Exfoliation of dull grey bark in irregular plates exposes inner bark, which varies from silver-blue to greenish-blue, to light brown, to whitish, to (in age) a chalky-white.''

The last describes *Pinus bungeana,* the Chinese Lace-bark Pine.

Not one of this list of pertinent facts is irrelevant although some have considerably more importance than do others. One fact alone counts: no one pine has *all* of the attributes listed; it is either one or the other in each category.

Many of the intricacies of comparative analysis as applied to the pine tree have now been reviewed. We shall soon have an opportunity, to apply our analytic systematics to pinelike trees (trees of other families and genera—all cone-bearing—but many of which are vastly different from pines) and, to have a hard look at the pines themselves.

Before going on into an even more stratified scientific procedure called "taxonomy," we must first, if briefly, mention some of the non-applicatory (i.e., to field identification) properties of the pine tree.

We have already agreed that the chemical properties, cellular fabrication, photosynthesis, respiration, nutrition, and the complexities of genetic structure are far more in the realm of botanical textbooks than in a field guide—for, in fact, the same complexities of structure and function will not only cover the pines, they will be virtually the same in any plant.

There are, however, properties of the pine that we should not overlook, such as fragrance, resin and wood.

FRAGRANCE

Fragrance can hardly be a comparative measure in telling one pine from another. The individual scents of Pine species may indeed be variable and even most poignantly so; but our noses are far lacking in the memory factor to render it into an applicatory usefulness.

Pine fragrance is apparently of far less complication chemically than, say, are flowers. If one should be oriented toward chemical knowledge, the fact that the fragrance of flowering plants is a complex blend of alcohols, esters, aldehydes, ketones, and many other oxygen-containing compounds, may be succinct and forthright by way of information. To one who is not so oriented, it means nothing.

The fragrance of pines comes from the needles and from the bark. In hot weather there is often a distinct bluish haze over pine forests, which comes from the exudation of essential oils through the stomata of the needles.

RESIN

Resin as it exudes from the tree, sticking to one's fingers or irrevocably staining the back of one's shirt, is another fragrant product of the pine. It is made from three substances: a volatile oil called turpentine; an amberlike substance called rosin; and chemical fixatives with high-boiling properties that, like perfume additives to hold that scent, make the resin—

particularly on warm days—even more fragrant and last-ing.

Turpentine itself is a familiar product to any househol-der. It is the *better* of the paint thinners and has many uses, as its continual disappearance from its cellar shelf will indicate. But the volatile oil of one pine is not the same as another; in fact, all one hundred of the existing pine species is said to have a different chemical combination in its terpenes. Most of the commercial supplies of turpentine in the United States come from the southern pine forests, most from the ''Big Four'' of timber trees: the Longleaf Pine, *Pinus palustris;* the Loblolly Pine, *Pinus taeda;* the Slash Pine, *Pinus elliottii;* and the Shortleaf Pine, *Pinus echinata.* We have become quite used to the fragrance of this product. However, the turpentine from the western Lodgepole Pine is grass-scented; others, like the Italian Stone Pine and the Ponderosa Pine are equally sweet and fragrant with the scents of limonene (bitter lemon) or carene (camphor-scented). Others, without terpenes, have the strong scent of pineapple or vanilla.

WOOD

Wood as a commercial entity, is an after-product to be consumed. And a *dendrochronologist* is a scientist who counts the rings of dead trees, literally a ''tree time-watcher.''

No one need be told that wood grows in concentric rings and that lean years and years of abundance may be seen in these visual indications of growth. Actually, Leonardo da Vinci was a dendrochronologist, or attempted to be. But that is not to say that it is either a simple study or a limited one. Modern techniques have given impetus to this science and its use in archaeology is increasing rapidly to pinpoint calendar dates of events or civilizations. It is now being used.

The living tree itself is structured in the following man-ner, as the sketch shows:

1. The outer *bark,* which can be quite thick at the base—to even four inches—while, of course, towards the top of the tree it thins most considerably.

2. The next layer is the soft, moist, protective inner bark, the *phloem,* which serves as con-ducting tissue to transport food from the leaves, where it is manufactured, to the other extremity, the roots.

22

3. The all-important *cambium* layer is next: only a few cells thick, but enclosing the entire tree from the roots to the tips of the highest branches, it is the reproductive center where new cells are being produced and pushed outward and inward. It is the region of growth.

4. Next is the light-colored *xylem,* the tissue that serves to conduct water and soluble nutrients upward from the soil to the leaves where they can be used in the photosynthetic process.

5. The greater center of the tree, a "library," now of old growth rings of nonfunctioning (except for support of the tree) dead tissue—the wood.

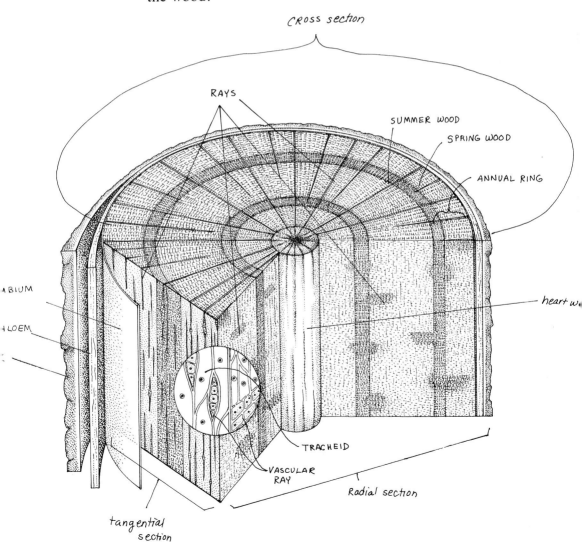

CROSS section

RAYS

SUMMER WOOD

SPRING WOOD

ANNUAL RING

A BIUM

HLOEM

heart w.

TRACHEID

VASCULAR RAY

Radial section

tangential section

It is remarkable to know that the living part of a tree is not unlike a coral reef—a small fraction only of living tissue protected in actuality by a dead skeleton. In a pine tree the entire portion of living cells comprises only one percent, or slightly more; the rest is just framework.

The nutrients from the soil are transported through the xylem tissue to the leaves, where they are incorporated into the food manufactured there. The food is transported downward to nourish the living, growing tissue—primarily the cambium—where reproduction and growth takes place. The dead and dying phloem tissue becomes bark on the outside; the dead and dying xylem becomes wood on the inside. Cells are multiplied and they, too, are dispersed—then replaced. Water and minerals course up and down, as well as do the essential pine oils, through a criss-crossed network of resin ducts and microscopic passages, in effect "lubricating" the living tissues wherein, in reaching into the xylem areas, they are sealed-off, functioning only where there is life.

The same tree, having been felled, bleeds its life away as water, resinous oils, nutrients and living cells drain out upon the ground or dry up. This tree—now still half-alive and green, many of its cells still living—is now "timber" and is hauled away, sawn into sections, and sold uncured, burned, or left to season.

Without wood man could scarcely exist; so the mention of wood-properties and timber-worth in our coverage of pines is an important part of it.

Basically, pines are all "soft wood" compared to the oaks, mahogonies, elms, walnuts, etc., which are substantially "hard woods" in every way. Amongst the pines, however, there are "soft pines," the so-called haploxylon pines and the "hard pines," diploxylon pines, which though harder and stringier than the former, are still "soft woods" to the industry or whoever physically works with the wood.

Identification is a matter of comparison. Whether it be among races of man, or of whales, or bats, or fishes, mosses, or trees—it is only by comparing one with others that physical identity can be made clear.

The scientific term for this comparative arrangement is *taxonomy*, which only means, simply enough, "arrangement in order," from the Greek words *taxis* (arrangement) and *vópos* (law). Since plants number in manifold thousands of orders, families, genera, species, and subdivisive tangential off-splittings, the subject can become wondrously confusing to a layperson. But yet, from the towering giants among the mist-filled Redwood forests to the least of papery-dry pines in some wind-blasted crevice in Outer Mongolia, each species is numbered, classified, and carefully arranged according to its similarities or dissimilarities, i.e., identity through physical and chemical comparisons.

However, in the making of comparisons, it must first be made clear with what or whom, and it is that with which we must deal.

A common name, so-called, is the use of the vernacular as opposed to the scientifically-oriented appellation. Scientific nomenclature is the only method by which accurate comparisons can be made, and without it there is only a slough of half-knowledge and misinterpretation.

For instance, reliance on "common names" such as "cedar," where a cedar may well not be a cedar, but a cypress; "pine" may not denote a pine at all but refer to a New Zealand Kauri; the common Red Cedar is a juniper. The Scotch fir—the true fir *(fur, fura)* of the old Norsemen—is not a fir but, botanically, a pine, *Pinus sylvestris*. Even worse, the Scotch Fir (pine) is nowhere more abundant than it is in the Scandinavian peninsula, and far less so in Scotland.

Taxonomy really began with Aristotle and Aristotle's pupil, Theophrastus (370-285 B.C.), and proceeded with increasing acceleration down to Pliny the Elder and Dioscorides in the first century A.D. It is now seen that the works of these early inquirers were often more accurate than "modern" versions in the eighteenth and nineteenth centuries. The reason for this is simply human carelessness; as stone bas-relief gave way to papyrus, as reed-paper became pulp and moveable type replaced calligraphy, more and more fools could parrot their often half-baked conclusions to a torpid public. Not that there was a paucity of truly scientific attempts at cohesion in all forms of naturalistic endeavor; there were earnest and forthright botanists and zoologists, always milling to the surface of the morass with yet-closer schemes, but still nothing emerged to cement a true direction in the matter of comparisons.

Finally, there arose in the mid-eighteenth century, Linnaeus, the name usually given to Carl von Linné, the Swedish botanist and student of Dr. Olaf Celsius, who began working out his complex classification—not in his native Swedish, but in a combination of mainly Greek and Latin, the classical languages of his day, and less susceptible to alteration because of its virtual cessation in the spoken language. In their classical forms—not always with the vulgate—both Latin and Greek are "pure;" any scholar can pronounce any name with little room for interpretation. Linnaeus' classification and language are as hard and fast as can be imagined and are as useful today as when he introduced them.

However, as the relatively simple work of Linnaeus has been seen to grow more complex under further scrutiny, the most distinguished of botanists would seem still to be embroiled in controversy as to rank and placement of conifers. There are some terms of reference amongst the adversaries such as "splitters," those who are inclined toward diversely individualistic breakdowns of species, and the "lumpers" who, conversely, prefer their own choice of holism in simplification. But none of this internecine confrontation need bother us, for not only are we assured that the most knowledgeable experts in the field are assiduous in their pursuit of these truths, but there is an international arbiter consisting of a Code, adopted at Montreal in 1959, and in Edinburgh in 1964, which serves as a safety valve for a too-zealous expansiveness in any direction.

The principal *taxa* (arithmetic groupings from holistic to miniscule) are:

NAME OF GROUP	ENDING	EXAMPLE
DIVISION	*-phyta*	*Spermatophyta*
CLASS	-opsida	*Coniferopsida*
ORDER	*-ales*	*Coniferales*
FAMILY	*-aceae*	*Pinaceae*
GENUS	*-a, x,*	*Pinus*, etc.
SPECIES	*-us, a,*	*Pinus nigra, um, sis, ii,*etc.
VARIETY	-var.	*Pinus nigra* var. *carmanica*

Note: And there can be groups, forms, subspecies, subgenera, etc. . . . and further complicated by hybrids (natural hybridization) or cultivari (propogated hybridization)

Turning all this up-side-down to simulate a "family tree," the chart, on pages 28–29, will show us where, precisely, pine trees fall into place amongst the conifers in general:

All of that does appear to be overwhelmingly indigestible, you will agree. But you cannot but be impressed that the subject of pines, about which hundreds of books and papers have been published, occupies so very small a niche in the overall view of cone-bearing trees. Also, you will find that it will all quickly fall into place as we go on. To bring it immediately closer to home: can it be possible that somewhere within a few miles of your house there is no juniper growing? Might there not be a *Cryptomeria* nearby—on an estate, or in a cemetery near your home? Does not your local florist or supermarket offer you a Norfolk Island Pine? The glen of last summer, where you fished for trout: hemlocks? The skier will know all about spruces. And Christmas after Christmas, from early childhood, haven't you known the incense of the fir?

You will know them because they have been a part of your life, these stiff, evergreen, almost impertinent sentinels, so often cultivated to lend dignity and aplomb to what frequently becomes an untidy sprawl of informality in deciduous plantings—yew hedges; spruce wind-walls; arbor vitae, ad nauseum in every direction; juniper columns (Have you ever seen an Irish juniper? You would not believe the flag-pole-compactness, the spearpointed apex, and the infinite *greenness* of its green! It is more a needle than a tree.); the tender green of larches, which, like forsythia, are so much a springtime thing; and, of course, the pines—pines of so many varied hues, textures, scents and profiles. The cast of characters in this book are hardly new to you; it is only that, together, we are trying to gather them all in so that, when we might wish to plant, cut, prune, build, beautify, or simply to have fun with identifying them, we can do it more easily and with a better concept of each in its relationship to another.

The interested layman might well be quite astonished, when first learning of it, by the yews being so isolated on the family tree. Yews are so ubiquitous and "pine-like," that one is inclined to lump them all together. But, however green and pleasant to the eye, yews have one decidedly "un-piney" characteristic; they are quite poisonous to certain animals. In England, for instance, where yews are widely planted and often used in topiary work, the clippings are carefully gathered and burned if the trees are anywhere bordering cattle enclosures or barnyards.

The Ginkgo (you may know it from parks) with its mothlike spreading leaves always a curiosity, is so different from any other tree that it must be classified as a separate *order,* having only one specie.

27

Fokiena
FOXIEN CEDAR
CHINA

Fitzroya
FITZROYA
CHILE & ARGENTINA

Diselma
DISELMA
TASMANIA

Cypressus
CYPRESSUS
N. TEMPERATE ZONE

XCupressocyparus
HYDRID CYPRESSUS
(ENGLAND)

Chamaecyparis
FALSE CYPRESS
N. TEMPERATE ZONE, N
& JAPAN

Calocedrus
INCENSE CEDAR
NORTH AMERICA, CHIN
FORMOSA

Callistrus
CYPRESS PINES
AUSTRALIA AND
TASMANIA

Austrocedrus
CHILIAN CEDAR
CHILE & ARGENTINA

Actinostrobus
AUSTRALIAN CEDAR
WESTERN AUSTRALIA

Taxodium
POND CYPRESS
SOUTHERN U.S.A.

Taiwania
TAIWANIA
FORMOSA

Sequoiadendron
GIANT SEQUOIA
CALIFORNIA, U.S.A.

Sequoia
SEQUOIA
COASTAL CALIFORNIA
U.S.A.

Sciadopitys
JAPANESE UMBRELLA
PINE
JAPAN

Metasequoia
DAWN REDWOOD
CHINA

Glyptostrobus
CHINESE DECIDUOUS
CYPRESS
CHINA

Cunninghamia
CUNNINGHAMIA
CHINA

Cryptomeria
JAPANESE CEDAR
JAPAN & CHINA

Athrotaxus
TASMANIAN CEDAR
TASMANIA

GENUS

Tsuga
HEMLOCKS
N. TEMP. ZONE,
N.A. & JAPAN

Pseudotsuga
DOUGLAS FIRS
N. TEMP. ZONE,
N.A. & JAPAN

Pseudolarix
GOLDEN LARCH
CHINA

Pinus
PINES
WORLDWIDE

Picea
SPRUCES
N. TEMP.
ZONE

Larix
LARCHES
N. TEMP. ZONE
TO ARCTIC

Keteleeria
PERE DAVID'S PINE
CHINA, FORMOSA

Cedrus
TRUE CEDARS
SYRIA, ATLASRD
CYPRUS

Cathaya (New)
(RESEMBLES SPRUCES
& FIRS)
CHINA

Abies
SILVER FIRS
N. TEMP. ZONE

Pineceae
PINE FAMILY

Taxodiaceae
DECIDUOUS
CYPRESS
FAMILY

Ginkgoales
THE GINKGO;
MAIDENHAIR TREE
(A SINGLE FAMILY
CONSISTING OF A
SINGLE TREE)

rus
PER
LDWIDE

drus
R-DROP CEDAR
ZEALAND &
CALEDONIA

llitropus
JDO-ARAUCARIA
GUINEA

cedrus
V GUINEA CEDAR
THERN CHILE

odendron
THERN CHILE

clinus
RACLINUS
GERIA, MOROCCO,
LTA

OR-VITAE
RTH TEMPERATE ZONE

pus
A ARBLE-VITAE
AN

ringtonia
PRESS PINES
JTH AFRICA

Saxegothaea
PRINCE ALBERTS YEW
CHILE & PATAGONIA

Podocarpus
YELLOW WOOD
S. HEMISPHERE

Phyllocladus
TOMTOA, OR CELERY-
TOPPED PINE
NEW ZEALAND

Microstrobus
ALPINE MICROSTROBUS
NEW ZEALAND, AUSTRALIA
TASMANIA

Microcachrys
ALPINE MICROCACHRYS
TASMANIA

Dacridium
MOUNTAIN PINE
AUSTRALASIA

Araucaria
NORFOLK IS.
PINE
S. HEMISPHERE.
AUST. S. AMER.

Acmopyle
NEW CALEDONIA
FHI

Agathis
KAURI PINES
NEW ZEALAND
AUSTRALIA

Cephalotaxus
COW'S TAIL PINE
CHINA, JAPAN,
VIETNAM

Podocarpaceae
PODOCARPUS
FAMILY

Cupressaceae
CYPRESS
FAMILY

Araucariaceae
MONKEY-PUZZLE
FAMILY

Cephalotaxoceae
PLUM-YEW
FAMILY

FAMILY

Coniferales
ORDER

Taxales
THE YEWS
(CONSISTING OF A
SINGLE FAMILY, *TAXACEAE*
WORLDWIDE

Coniferopsida
(CONE-BEARING
PLANTS)
CLASS

Spermatophyta
(SEED-BEARING
PLANTS)
DIVISION

The Gingko is the principal sacred tree of the Far East, planted near every temple and palace, and the edible seeds are a well-known commercial item in Japanese and Chinese towns, being consumed in huge amounts at times of feasting to (it is believed) lessen the effects of wine. Also, in New York City in the autumn, certain of the Chinese community collect from the city's parks and avenues the grey-pink fruit. They put the pulpy ball between the palms of their hands and rub off the pulp to get at the kernel, an edible nut the size of a standard pea.

The Plum-yew family with its single genus *Cephalotaxus,* is oriental, and resembles a yew but with longer, less stiff leaves. It has little economic value.

The Podocarpus Family is confined to the Southern Hemisphere where it is largely found in the mountain forests of both warm temperate zones and in the superheated tropics. The wood is a valuable economic commodity and the popular name for most species is Yellow Wood, for the freshly-cut timber is a vivid yellow though it later turns brownish on exposure to air. The seven genera comprising the family vary considerably—from the Toatoa, or Celery-topped Pine, which I have seen on the North Island of New Zealand in alpine locations, to the looming giants I saw felled in the steaming rain forests of Cape York in Australia.

The Monkey-Puzzle Family, the common name botanically accepted for the *Araucariaceae* is a prime example of how at complete random has been the appellative procedure in this branch of science. These great evergreen trees are native to the Southern Hemisphere and are impressive in their grandeur, but the name is said to have originated in Cornwall, England, where a friend remarked to a botanist, in possession of a young tree, that, "It would puzzle a monkey to climb that tree," and the owner straightway adopted the name and it appears, feigning dignity, in every botanical listing of the family, generally equally puzzling, those who first see it. Of the two genera, *Araucaria* takes its name (with considerably more sense) from the province of Arauco in southern Chile, but it is much more commonly known by the name of the Norfolk Island Pine; while *Agathis* (named, again sensibly) from the Greek, meaning "a ball of thread," in reference to the globose cones) comprises the beautiful Kauri Pines (of course they are not true pines at all) of New Zealand and Australia. Both genera are useful as timber and are great, tall trees, but their greatest attraction is in their unique symmetry and beauty of proportion.

The evergreen Cypress Family, the *Cupressaceae*, is the largest of all in numbers of genera and varies most considerably. The family includes the columnar junipers; the incense cedar of Formosa; the Cypress "Pines" of South Africa; the much-planted Arbor vitae, often called the White Cedar in many parts of the United States. Cypresses generally possess decorative merit and their timber is useful and durable. Some genera are ubiquitous and worldwide in distribution, while others are rare and obscure. Many are aromatic, some pleasingly so, while others are decidedly repelling. The hardy *Juniperus*, well-known for its tenacity in clinging to scant soils, is mostly of small to medium size, tough and rugged, while the *Chamaecyparis*, the False Cypress of Formosa and Oregon attains heights of over 200 feet with a girth of over 20 feet or more.

The deciduous Cypress Family, *Taxodiaceae*, is perhaps the most imposing family of all the *Coniferopsida*, for it contains the greatest, most magnificent trees on earth, the Giant Sequoia or California Redwood, *Sequoia sempervirens*, and *Sequoiadendron giganteum*, the Big Tree. These trees are among the oldest in the world (*the* oldest is a pine) and are a heritage of generations unborn—a heritage that is, today, being ravaged and depleted by the greed and shortsightedness of certain commercial ventures that insist, because of the enduring quality of its wood, upon its transformation from the greatest of natural wonders in its mist-shrouded California hills, into bird feeders, porch furniture, and into tasteless modern structure. "Redwood," as it is called, is not to be confused with the "redwood" of European commerce, *Pinus sylvestris*.

Others of this remarkable family are *Taxodium*, the flare-bolled swamp cypress of the southeastern United States—which is, to many Americans, the typification of "cypress;" *Metasequoia*, the Dawn Redwood of China, a "living fossil," undiscovered until 1945; *Sciodopitys*, the Japanese Umbrella Pine, so unique and valuable to arborists; *Cunninghamia*, the Chinese Fir, in China known as the most useful wood next to bamboo, which is used to build junks, houses, and, of all things, coffins—the latter because of its enduring nature and fragrant scent; and *Cryptomeria*, the ornamental Japanese Cedar.

Finally, we reach the Pine Family, the *Pinaceae*.

Now on "home ground," we can quickly review the rare and limited genera; *Cathaya*, of China, which resembles the spruces and firs; *Keteleeria*, or Père David's Pine, also

Chinese, resembling a silver fir; and the deciduous *Pseudolarix,* the Golden Larch, again, from China, that resembles a larch but differs from it by its wide leaves, club-shaped shoots, and perishable cones (i.e., the cones break up and crumble upon attaining ripeness). Also, *Pseudotsuga,* the Douglas Fir, covers immense areas of the Pacific coastal regions of the United States and Canada. The beauty and dignity and usefulness of this large and valuable tree cry out for more detailed coverage, but it, as well as those mentioned above, must, in effect, be summarily dismissed for this is a book about pines, not about pseudo-pines.

However, the remaining genera standing in our way of progress must be covered with something more of recognition, because it is they, which, more often than any others of the conifers, are to be confused with pines. They are: the Firs, Spruces, Larches, Hemlocks and Cedars (the juxtapositioning is my own).

Douglas Fir & cone

FIRS

Firs, *Abies,* are evergreen, aromatic, "soft" (in comparison to spruces and many pines, which can be "stiff") tender, and altogether satisfactory. They are found only in the North Temperate Zone—but whether from Afghanistan, Bhutan, the hills of Sweden, the eastern slopes of the White Mountains in New England, or covering the lofty crags of the Canadian Rockies, the many (nearly 200 species and varieties) *Abies* are all clean, i.e., demanding-of and prospering only in clean air, generally subalpine, but descending much lower in favorable conditions, and tall, stately, and (again) soft. Less poetically, they have whorled branches; flat, needlelike (but soft) leaves, flat or flattish with distinct resin canals that leave a disclike scar when they fall. Erect cones ripen in one year and shed scales and bracts along with seeds at maturity. The leaves are generally silvery grey-green, often very light (whitish) on the ventral side. Fir wood is less competitive in quality to pine, being often knotty and tough, but it is a valuable commercial item.

Sitka Spruce & cone

SPRUCES

Picea are stiff, staunch, rugose, hardy and (like the firs) eminently satisfactory. Spruces are less demanding than firs, often prospering on poor, wet land upon which pines cannot thrive. They are able to withstand extreme exposure and stiffly offer themselves as excellent wind-breaks. The wood is soft, odorless, long-fibered, often with loose knots, but gener-

32

ally is more useful than fir. They are distinguished from firs by their woody, peglike leaf bases that remain on the branches after the needles have fallen, and by the pendulous cones that remain intact when ripe. Seeds are quite small and winged. Spruces are sharp to the touch; firs, soft. Spruces are to be distinguished from pines by the numerous, sheathless, needlelike small leaves that uniformly cover a branch after the fashion of a hairbrush, two, three, or five within a sheath. Cones ripen in two to three years, and are woody with lasting scales. The seed wing is large, as a rule, but can be miniscule or even absent.

LARCHES

Larches, *Larix*, are, first of all, completely deciduous, losing all of their many thousands of fine needles each year and growing them back on the same branches the following spring. They are valued as ornamentals because, with the advent of spring there is, first, a faint greenish blush developing with time into an almost feathered appearance. Also, the green of the larches is always light and joyous and stands in vivid contrast to their often sombre cone-bearing relatives. In addition, after darkening only slightly during the heat of summer, with the coming of autumn the larch needles turn a golden hue before a hard frost causes them to drop.

The wood of the larch is strong and hard, coarsegrained and durable. It was often used for the masts of nordic ships and it has lasting qualities that make it most useful for railway sleepers and for fencing.

The leaves are needlelike but soft and deciduous; they are tufted onto short spurs and scattered on long shoots. The cones are globular, woody, and ripen in one year. Seeds are small and winged.

In essence, the larch is always light and feathery in foliage but seemingly dead in winter as its slender naked branches form a dark lacework against the sky.

American Larch & cone

HEMLOCK

Tsuga thrives along the damp corridors of mountain brooks and rocky defiles where the soil is dark and loamy and always moist—the home (in America) of the Indian Pipe and the Red-backed Vole. The leaves are dark green, aromatic, usually blunt, and flat on the branches. Hemlocks can be large, 60 to 100 feet high. Cones are small and solitary. The wood is soft and inclined toward being knotty and to splinter

Eastern Hemlock & cone

Cedar of Lebanon & cone

and is used generally for boxes, pulp, and inferior building purposes . Hemlocks are worldwide in distribution through the North Temperate Zone. (To set the record straight: the famous "hemlock" that Socrates drank was not related to *Tsuga,* but was from a biennial herb of the carrot family, *Conium maculatum,* which, when distilled is a virulent poison. Even worse for Socrates, *Conium Maculatum* "emits a disagreeable smell like mice.")

CEDAR

"True Cedar" is nearly always used in the vernacular because of the universality of applying the name to species in many genera amongst different families. Usually,—at least in America—the term "cedar" is given to the juniper, "Red Cedar," or to the White Cypress *(Chamaecyparis thyoides)* "White Cedar." *True* cedars, then, are only of the genus *Cedrus* and are native only to the Island of Cyprus, the Atlas Mountains, the mountains of Syria, and the Himalayas. The biblical "cedars of Lebanon" are true cedars.

Cedrus is much in appearance like *Larix* in the tufted masses of its needles but, very unlike *Larix,* it is evergreen. Cones are large, erect, and barrel-shaped and are disseminated by wet weather after releasing their broad-winged seeds. The wood is oily and sweet-scented and is an important local timber in its native habitat. It is said that over 70 different kinds of wood—not one of them cedars—are called "cedar" with one term or another as a prefix. *Cedrus* has been transplanted worldwide because of the beauty of its massive trunks and large, spreading branches when mature. Trees of this genus, however, are pyramidal in form when young.

PINES

The Genus *Pinus*
Subgenera: *Haploxylon, Diploxylon*

Pines are the oldest genus in the entire family *Pinaceae,* which we have reviewed in order to find out what a pine is *not.* Certain of the genera we have covered; some, in the *Pinaceae,* and others in other families, are weak, somnolent, or senescent; some are even slowly disappearing. Pines, on the contrary, are still vigorously advancing, occupying new territories by the simple expediency of "new blood," i.e., stronger varieties and hybrids more adaptable to a world now being changed chemically as well as physically. Crossbreeding occurs among many species in the genera we have already covered but in *Pinus* we shall have to look more closely.

Until now we have been dealing only with the basic Linnaean classification, each having only a generic and specific name. This type of binomial taxonomy is called "classical, conventional, or descriptive taxonomy." Within these limits there are "good" species, those clearly identifiable either because of their isolation or because they are less inclined toward intercrossing. And there are "bad" species of which the exact opposite is true. With Linnaean classification the taxonomy of pines was based on external morphology. Basically, modern taxonomy still is—but there have arisen varied approaches to the essential question of which species intercross and which do not.

Linnaeus had given us binomial nomenclature: the genus *Pinus* is "Pine"; the species *strobus,* is what *kind* of pine; the *varieties* of *strobus* are those to which *strobus* is inclined to vary toward under different conditions, but *strobus* is still *strobus*. George Engelmann, in 1880, went further than anyone before him in investigating flowers, pollen grains, vascular bundles of needles, and the presence or absence of "strengthening cells" around the resin canals; and he added these considerations to the hitherto more simple morphological approach. E. Koehne, in 1893, used the cross section of needles to divide the genus into two subgenera. Shaw, in 1914, applied his work on the position of resin canals and the rays of wood-structure to differentiate the species.

Morphological characteristics still play the most substantial role in the classification of pines, but modern-day technological advances have introduced other approaches which are now widely employed. They are, briefly: the *Genetic Approach,* in which the complexities of hybridization and the chromosomal breakdowns are weighed; the *Geographical Approach,* in which species previously separated by distance are, once in proximity, seen either to intercross or not to intercross; the *Physioecological Approach,* in which variations of temperature, soil conditions, aridity, disease, fires, predation, etc., are stressed; the *Paleobotanical Approach,* where the discovery and interpretation of fossil species lead to certain reconsideration in the relationships of certain species; and, finally, the *Chemical Approach,* wherein the inherent chemical containments of pine, such as alkaloids, polyphenols, and cyclitols, are used to help compare one species with another.

When Koehne separated the genus *Pinus* into two subgenera, he gave them the names *haploxylon,* for those pines of which a cross section of the needles shows but one vascular bundle and *diploxylon* for those containing two bundles. According to Mirov, the two subgenera can also always be distinguished by "the scarious bracts subtending the short shoots. In haploxylon pines, the bract is non-recurrent," (botanically: not descending downward) "and thus the branches are smooth. In diploxylon pines, the bract is decurrent, causing the branches to be rough."

.   Koehne coined the names from Greek "haploos," meaning single, and "diploos," double. He was the first to use the terms and others, following, chose to honor Koehne by keeping his terms or *not* to honor him by ignoring them. Mirov has chosen to follow Koehne and retains the subgenera under Koehne's terminology, and you will find that here, in listing *Pinus* species, the subgeneric divisions are retained (following Mirov) and no attempt is made to translate Koehne into simpler terms. At this point it might be considered an excellent opportunity to explain the difference between this, an interpretive introduction to a subject, *mainly pictorial,* and any definitive work such as, for example, Mirov's principal contribution on the pines, *The Genus Pinus,* or Dallimore, Jackson, and Harrison's *Handbook of Coniferae and Ginkgoaceae.* It is not our role to formulate scientific theory but only to interpret its often complex structure and translate it into a more readily understandable format. The immediate purpose is none other than to build a bridge between you, the interested layperson, and *scientific* authority. It is to *them* to whom you must look for definitive expansion in depth.

The following is a listing of all known species of pines, by region and by specific and varietal separation.

Eastern America
(North of Mexico)

Haploxylon Pines

Pinus strobus Linn.
Eastern White Pine

Diploxylon Pines

Pinus banksiana Lamb.	*Pinus pungens* Lamb.
Jack Pine	Table-mountain Pine
Pinus clausa (Chap.) Vasey	*Pinus resinosa* Ait.
Sand Pine	Red Pine

Pinus echinata Mill.
Shortleaf Pine

Pinus elliottii Engel.
Slash Pine

Pinus glabra Walt.
Spruce Pine

Pinus palustris Mill.
Longleaf Pine

Pinus rigida Mill.
Pitch Pine

Pinus serotina Michx.
Pond Pine

Pinus taeda Linn.
Loblolly Pine

Pinus virginiana Mill.
Virginia Scrub Pine

Western America

(North of Mexico)

Haploxylon Pines

Pinus albicaulis Engel.
White-bark Pine

Pinus aristata Engel.
Bristle-cone Pine

Pinus balfouriana Balf.
Foxtail Pine

Pinus edulis Enge
Two-leaved Nut Pine

Pinus flexilis James
Limber Pine

Pinus lambertiana Dougl.
Sugar Pine

Pinus monophylla Torr.
Single-leaf Pine

Pinus monticola Dougl.
Western White Pine

Pinus quadrifolia Sud.
Four-leaved Nut Pine

Diploxylon Pines

Pinus attenuata Lemmon
Knob-cone Pine

Pinus contorta Dougl.
Lodgepole Pine

Pinus coulteri D. Don
Big-cone Pine

Pinus jeffreyi Grev. & Balf.
Jeffrey's Pine

Pinus muricata D. Don
Obispo Pine

Pinus ponderosa Laws.
Ponderosa Pine

Pinus radiata D. Don
Monterey Pine

Pinus sabiniana Dougl.
Digger Pine

Pinus torreyana Parry
Torrey Pine

Pinus washoensis Mason
& Stockwell
Washoe Pine

Mexico
(And most of Central America)

Haploxylon Pines

Pinus ayacahuite Ehrenburg
    Mexican White Pine

Pinus cembroides Zucc.
    Pinon Pine

Pinus culminicola And.
& Beam.
    (No English name)

Pinus nelsonii Shaw
    Nelson Pine

Pinus pinceana Gord.
    Pince's Pine

Pinus strobiformis Engelm.
    (No English name)

Pinus strobus Linn. var.
chiapenis
    Chiapes Pine

Diploxylon Pines

Pinus arizonica Engelm.
    Arizona Pine

Pinus chihuahuana Engelm.
    Chihuahua Pine

Pinus cooperii Blanco
    Cooper's Pine

Pinus douglasiana Martinez
    (No English name)

Pinus durangensis Martinez
    Durango Pine

Pinus engelmannii Carr.
    Apache Pine

Pinus greggii Engelm.
    Gregg's Pine

Pinus hartweggii Lindl.
    Hartweg Pine

Pinus herrerai Martinez
    (No English name)

Pinus lawsonii Roezl
    Lawson's Pine

Pinus leiophylla Sch.
& Deppe
    Smoothleaved Pine

Pinus lumholtzii Rob & Fern.
    Lumholtz Pine

Pinus michoacana Martinez
    (No English name)

Pinus montezumae Lamb.
    Montezuma Pine

Pinus oaxacana Mirov
    (No English name)

Pinus oocarpa Schiede
    (No English name)

Pinus patula Schl. & Cham.
    Jelecote Pine

Pinus pringlei Shaw
    Pringle Pine

Pinus pseudostrobus Lindl.
    False White Pine

Pinus rudis Endl.
    (No English name)

Pinus tenuifolia Benth
    (No English name)

Pinus teocote Schl. & Cham.
    Aztec Pine

Caribbean Area, Southern Florida, Eastern Central America

Haploxylon Pines

None

Diploxylon Pines

Pinus caribaea Morelet
Caribbean Pine

Pinus cubensis Grisebach
Cuban Pine

Pinus elliottii var. *densa*, Little & Dor.
Florida Slash Pine

Pinus occidentalis Swartz
Cuban Pine

Pinus tropicalis Morelet
(No English name)

Mediterranean Area

Haploxylon Pines

Pinus cembra Linn.
Swiss Stone Pine

Pinus peuce Grisebach
Balkan Pine

Diploxylon Pines

Pinus brutia Ten.
Calabrian Pine

Pinus canariensis Smith
Canary Pine

Pinus eldarica Medw.
(No English name)

Pinus halepensis Mill.
Aleppo Pine

Pinus heldreichii Christ.
Heldreich Pine

Pinus montana Mill.
Swiss Mountain Pine; Mugo Pine

Pinus nigra Arn.
Australian Pine

Pinus pinaster Ait.
Cluster or Maritime Pine

Pinus pinea Linn.
Italian Stone Pine; Umbrella Pine

Pinus pityusa Steven
Pitzunda Pine

Northern Eurasia

Haploxylon Pines

Pinus pumila Regel
Japanese Stone Pine

Pinus sibirica Mayr
Siberian Pine

Diploxylon Pines

Pinus sylvestris Linn.
Scotch Pine

Southeastern Asia

Haploxylon Pines

Pinus armandi Franchet
Chinese White Pine

Pinus wallichiana Jackson
Himalayan White Pine

Pinus bungeana Zucc.
Lace-bark Pine

Pinus parviflora Sieb. & Zucc.
Japanese White Pine

Pinus dalatensis de Ferre
(No English name)

Pinus koraiensis Sieb. & Zucc.
Korean Pine

Pinus fenzeliana Hand.-Maz.
(No English name)

Pinus kwangtungensis Chun
(No English name)

Pinus gerardiana Wall.
Ghilghoza Pine

Pinus morrisonicola Hayata
(No English name)

Pinus pentaphylla Mayr
Japanese White Pine

Diploxylon Pines

Pinus densiflora Sieb. & Zucc.
Japanese Red Pine

Pinus khasya Royle
Khasia Pine

Pinus funebris Komarov
(No English name)

Pinus luchuensis Mayr
Okinawa Pine

Pinus hwangshanensis Hsia
(No English name)

Pinus massoniana Lamb.
Masson Pine

Pinus insularis Endl.
Luzon Pine

Pinus merkusii De Vriese
Merkus Pine

Pinus roxburghii Sar.
 Chir Pine

Pinus taiwanensis Hayata
 Formosa Pine

Pinus tabulaeformis Carr.
 Chinese Pine

Pinus thunbergii Parl.
 Japanese Black Pine

Pinus yunnanensis Franchet
 Yunnan Pine

Thus, having seen yet another complicated display of names, we are faced with the decision of how best to approach the actual identification of pines. There are many authorities, as we have discussed, who offer their own versions. Many of them are thorough, though some are ponderous. This is basically an introductory field guide and, as has been stated, it is principally a picture-book; i.e., one *should* be able to "look at the pictures" and identify any pine. It is hoped that that will often be the case but, still, we are faced with a certain amount of inescapable non-conformity in dealing with trees; field identification is never that easy. We have included as lengthy and as detailed information as space will permit, but also we must have a *key,* for no single picture can cover every detail. This key we have chosen to lift from the body of the text and to place where it can be more readily used as a reference. Also, where any pine is to be found in the Arthur Ross Pinetum, I have indicated this by the addition of an asterisk located below the key and, as well, a notation of at what date the species was first known to be introduced to cultivation. In addition, besides the detailed illustrations, there has been an attempt, in the more important of the described species, to show the form and character of the tree in a smaller black-and-white drawing, as well as some random drawings to perhaps further aid in recognition.

   In the section following, illustrated in color, are pines that are to be found in the Arthur Ross Pinetum, from which base we started. This method of approach was chosen because, in a labeled pinetum, with book in hand, one has a far better chance of introductory success in a known situation than in an unknown situation. It is simply a composite learning device, as a zoological park is an excellent beginning for the use of a field guide to the birds or other animals. Of course, any pinetum or arboretum will suffice, or a park system, or, failing any of these, one can jump to the ultimate goal of stopping by the roadside and seeking the identity of any feral pine.

Again, geographic distribution is the principal basis of systematics here used in the separation of Pine species. Secondarily, the species are broken down into *haploxylon* (simple pines) or *diploxylon* (complex pines). Beyond that, alphabetic consideration *under its specific name* is used to facilitate easy search within the bounds of geographic grouping. For use as a field guide it must only be remembered that worldwide transplantation makes the keys the only concrete platform for accurate identification.

Eastern North American Pines

PINUS BANKSIANA
Jack Pine

Named for Sir Joseph Banks (1743-1820), President of the Royal Society and virtual director of the Royal Botanical Gardens, Kew, the most northerly of American pines, *Pinus banksiana* covers much of the Canadian forest belt and reaches well into the tundra, often growing on the most tenuous of scant soil over perpetual ice. The Jack Pine is tough, gnarled, rugose, dark, forbidding and relatively worthless. Even its cones are curved and warped. It is a scrubby, scruffy, terrierlike tree, clinging to the barren lands in defiance of weather and sparsity of nutrients. Often low and bushlike, it can rise as high as 70 feet, but it is more often found to be scraggly and crooked, little over 20 feet tall, covering vast expanses of northern wastelands. Its southern extent reaches only to northern New York, northern New England, and to Minnesota and Michigan.

One fascinating item, to counterbalance the monotonous saga of the Jack Pine, is the not quite symbiotic—but nearly so—relationship of this tree and the rare Kirtland's Warbler. This small, brightly-painted bird is also known as the Jack Pine Warbler. This bird nests—in all the world—only in dense stands of young *Pinus banksiana,* 3 to 18 feet tall, within an area limited to 60 by 80 miles of the central plains of Michigan. The birds, sheltered by these pines, feed almost entirely on the insects they find in the pine branches and never stray from these trees until they migrate each autumn to the Bahamas—from which islands, with the arrival of spring, they return to the same Jack Pines, and usually within sight of their last year's nest.

Sometimes the Jack Pine is planted as a binder in areas of dry and sandy soil, but it can hardly be described as ornamental. It is said that, in a natural state, the cones open only after the high heat of a forest fire. Its wood is often soft, brittle, weak, and of little use, but, depending upon its situation, it can produce a wood approaching that of the Red Pine *(P. resinosa)* in hardness. Formerly ignored, now in these

Juck
banksiana

PINUS BANKSIANA *Jack Pine*

days of wood-scarcity, the Jack Pine is often squeezed-in amongst lumber of better quality and sold in some quantity.

Pinus banksiana is easily identified within its range by its short needles, crooked branches, and by its considerably warped and crooked cones; the latter being most irregular in form, varying from ovoid-conic, to oblique, and curved to nearly a semi-circle in extreme instances. The cones are tawny-yellow on exposed parts while the apex is often of two distinct shades. The conal scales are rhomboidal and spineless, and open irregularly to gradually spread the seeds. Often the cones remain unopened for many years before distribution takes place.

KEY

Needles: 2 to a sheath; olive-green ("black" in the distance) stiff, curved, or slightly twisted; ¾-1½" long, rudimentary teeth on margins, blunt-pointed apex, marginal resin canals; basal sheath ⅛" long.

Cones: Irregularly curved or warped; oval-shaped; 1¼-2½" long, ½-1" wide at base; lustrous tawny yellow, "like peanuts," without prickle, often staying unopened on branches for many years.

Branches: Upward-growing in youth, yellowish to purplish-brown, slender, but tough.

Bark: Reddish-brown to purplish, with deep fissures forming narrow ridges.

Introduced: 1783

PINUS ECHINATA *Shortleaf Pine*

PINUS ECHINATA
Shortleaf Pine

One of the "Big-Four" of the great southern timber trees, along with the Longleaf Pine *(P. palustris);* the Slash Pine *(P. elliottii);* and the Loblolly Pine *(P. taeda), Pinu echinata* covers thousands of square miles of the southeastern United States from the Gulf of Mexico to West Virginia, and even New York State, west to Texas.

The coarse-grained wood is strong and heavy with well-developed resin ducts and is used for whatever of general building and carpentry use where a sturdy pine can be utilized.

The Shortleaf Pine will grow to from 80-100 feet in height and will flourish on any sandy, gravelly soil that is well-drained, but it does not reach its most valuable proportions for 90-100 years. It is a "yellow-wood" pine, as are the others in its group.

Among the many birds that frequent its monotonous stands is the Pine Warbler, *Dendroica pinus,* which nests in these trees and which has a "creeping" or gliding walk as it searches for tiny insects hidden in the short-leaved branches.

Above all, this pine is principally distinguished from its related neighbors by the length of its needles which, compared to the others, are short-leaved. *Echinata* means "covered with prickles."

KEY

Needles: 2 to a sheath; deciduous every 2-5 years; dark, bluish-green, 3-5″ long; flexible and slender and slightly twisted; margins finely toothed; median resin canals and with a short, horny point.

Cones: 1½-2″ long; ovoid on very short stalks; grey-brown and with short—sometimes deciduous—prickle; remain on branches after seeds are dispersed; seeds, small and mottled with ½″ long reddish wing.

Branches: Young shoots pale green flushed with violet; older branches turning brown and with rough hairs at base of sheaths.

Bark: ¾-1″ thick; reddish, and divided into irregular plates.

Introduced: 1726

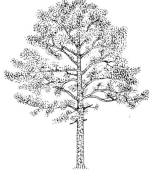

Shortleaf / echinata

PINUS PALUSTRIS
Longleaf Pine

"Longleaf"—needles up to eighteen inches—is certainly the most distinguishing characteristic of this beautiful pine. This tree, named *palustris* because it will grow in damp as well as sandy soil, is tall and straight—to 120 feet—except for a branched crown. Another of the "Big-Four" of southern yellow-woods it has great commercial value in the sturdiness and strength (an elasticity of 1,540,000 lbs per square inch) of its wood. The timber of this tree is often used as the standard of comparison for other soft woods. Further statistics show: strength in cross-breaking, 10,900 lbs per square inch; strength in compression, 6,850 lbs per square inch; and strength in tension, 15,200 lbs per square inch. The microscopic content of the wood of all of the "Big-Four," however, is so uniform that it is virtually impossible to identify them so that, in industrial use, they are nearly always intermixed as "yellow-wood pine" and share a worldwide reputation for excellence.

The Longleaf Pine, however, although so strong and durable in the quality of its work, is of less hardy constitution in its youthful growth and is not to be found further north than Virginia.

KEY

Longleaf/Palustris

Needles:	3 to a sheath; bright green and crowded on the branches; slender and flexible, to 18 inches long on youthful and vigorous trees but diminishing in length on older trees to one half that size; margins finely-toothed, median resin canals; basal sheath 1 inch long.
Cones:	Cylindrical or oblong-conic; 6-10 inches long, 2-3″ wide; dull brown with a sharp prickle; seed, ½″ long with a 1½″ wing.
Branches:	Young shoots orange-brown with prominent ridges; older branches gnarled and twisted.
Bark:	Reddish-brown and fissured.
Introduced:	1727

Patricia J. Wynne

PINUS PALUSTRIS
Longleaf Pine

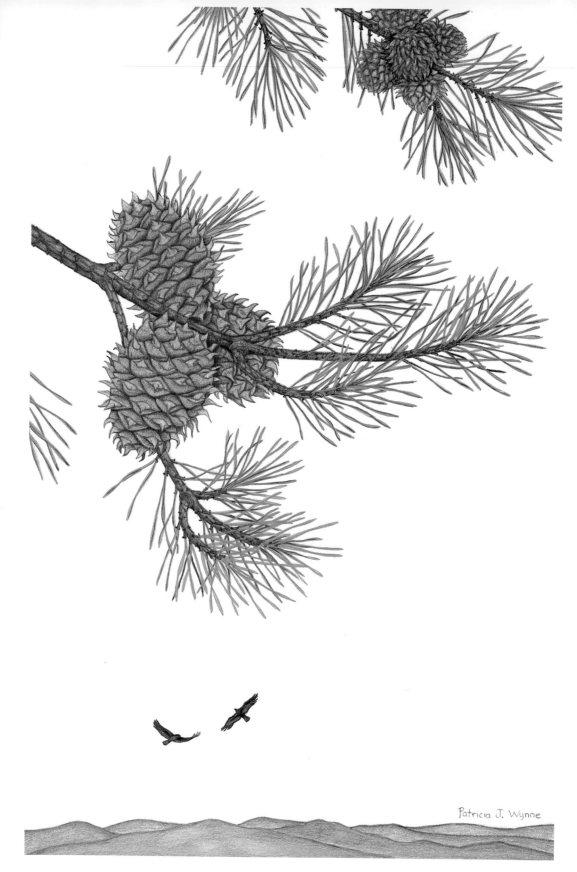

PINUS PUNGENS *Table Mountain Pine or Poverty Pine*

PINUS PUNGENS
Table Mountain Pine or Poverty Pine

Table Mountain is in the state of Tennessee but *P. pungens* covers a wide area of the American South from New Jersey to Georgia, growing in hilly areas on impoverished, worn-out, and generally rocky and worthless land. Also known as the "Poverty Pine" it is, itself, relatively worthless, having coarse-grained, knotty, and brittle wood. Into the bargain it is ugly and of nondescript proportion, dull, and stunted (generally only from 20-30 feet high). It is of perhaps some value in bringing completely wasted areas to at least a semblance of rejuvenation, preparing the land for the advent of more useful trees. Even its prickle is strongly-hooked and vicious, and much in evidence, as are the teeth of a lowly and mean cur dog. *Pungens* means "sharp-pointed," and refers to these prickles.

The Turkey Vulture, *Cathartes aura,* is a suitable denizen of the scraggly forests of the Poverty Pine.

Pinus pungens can be distinguished from other two-needled pines by its stout, rigid, sharp-pointed needles, by its cylindrical buds, by its branches bearing lateral buds and cones, and by its shining, reddish-brown bark.

KEY

Needles: 2 to a sheath (though sometimes three); persisting 3 years, crowded on the branches; dark, dull green, rigid and twisted, 2-3″ long; sharp-pointed with median resin canals; persistant basal sheath.

Cones: Solitary or in pairs; ovoid; bright brown; 1½-3″ long; armed with a strong, hooked spine; seed triangular, light brown.

Branches: Young shoots greenish, becoming reddish-brown. Branches rough and gnarled.

Bark: Reddish-brown and scaly.

Introduced: 1804

pungens / TABLE MT.

PINUS RESINOSA
Red Pine—Norway Pine

The Red Pine is native from Nova Scotia to Pennsylvania and westward through the northern tier of states to Minnesota and Manitoba.

This pine is often short of trunk and has a heavily-branched and thickly-leaved top when found growing in the open; but in the forest, where it is more often seen, it looms triumphantly skyward into the realm of the Red-tailed Hawk, *Buteo jamaicensis,* and is devoid of branches for fully three-fourths of its height. The tree is said to be more resistant to diseases than is *P. strobus.* The bark is pinkish-brown, thick and well-grooved by prominent fissures. The leaf clusters are dense and of a lighter, more bluish-green than those of the White Pine.

The wood is heavier and with more obvious resin ducts than the White Pine *(P. strobus);* its sapwood is cream-colored with clearly delineated annual rings, while the heartwood is a pinkish golden-yellow that turns darker in contact with air. It is straight-grained and harder and stronger than that of *P. strobus.* Ordinarily strong and hardy, this wood is quickly vulnerable to rot if placed in the earth without the protection of a preservative. It is widely used in construction, cabinetry, and boat-building, and is an important commercial product in ornamental use.

This tall and stately pine has a single, well-known variety, *P. resinosa* var. *globosa;* a dense, globular dwarf, discovered in New Hampshire around 1910. It often resembles *P. nigra* in this form, but is easily distinguished by its flexible leaves and marginal canals.

KEY

Red / Resinosa

Needles:	2 to a sheath; 4-6″ long; deciduous 4-5 years; flexible and slender, but more "wire-like" than *P. strobus;* more of a bluish-green; long basal sheaths and marginal resin canals.
Cones:	Delicate and conical; 1½-2½″ long; solitary or in pairs; no stalk; deciduous 2-4 years; light brown; seeds dark brown, ⅛″ long with ¾″ wing.
Branches:	Orange-brown, often with a silvery cast.
Bark:	Pinkish-brown; prominent, wide-waled, but shallow fissures.
Introduced:	1756

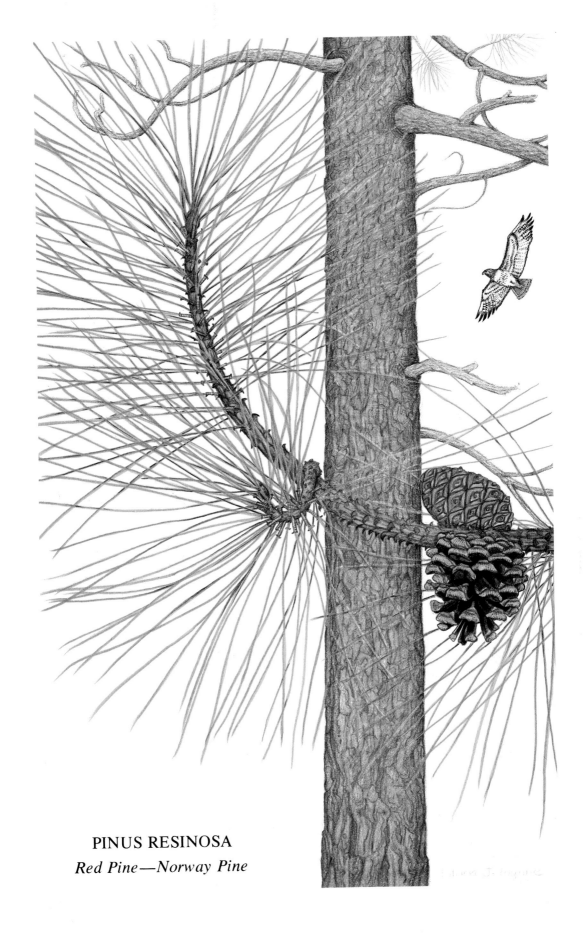

PINUS RESINOSA

Red Pine—Norway Pine

PINUS RIGIDA *Pitch Pine*

Patricia J. Wynne

PINUS RIGIDA
Pitch Pine

Another "poverty-type" pine, *Pinus rigida* has little to commend it, either commercially or by way of outward beauty. At very best, it can be said that, with age, because of its irregular and variable shapes, it can be picturesque. As with the others of its type, this tree is mostly found to be scrubby and stunted although, in some favorable situations, it will rise to over fifty feet.

This tree is often host to the wood-boring Pine Sawyer Beetle, *Monochamus notatus,* as well as to the Pine-Flower Snout Beetles, the *Nemonychidae,* which feed on the staminate flowers of pines.

The wood is knotty, and heavily resinous, of decidedly inferior quality, and is virtually worthless except for firewood.

This pine overlaps the ranges of both *P. pungens* and *P. virginiana.* All are of a scraggly type, less than regular in outline, and monotonous within their habitats. This pine is immediately separated from the other two by its three-needled sheaths and by its distinctly yellow-green aspect compared with other pines.

KEY

Needles: 3 to a sheath; deciduous every 2 years; 3½-4" long, stiff, rigid, twisted, yellow-green; finely-toothed margins; medium resin canals.

Cones: 1½-3½" long, sometimes cluster around branch; light brown, ovoid; transverse keel and recurved prickle; seeds dark brown, ¼" long with ¾" wing.

Branches: Young shoots green at first, becoming dull orange-brown; spreading branches from a conical crown.

Bark: Grey-brown to red-brown, deeply and irregularly fissured.

Introduced: 1713

pitch
rigida

PINUS STROBUS
Eastern White Pine

The Eastern White Pine is the great timber tree of the northeastern United States and is the State Tree of Maine. *P. strobus* is the largest pine in the United States next to California's Sugar Pine, *P. lambertiana,* and was "King of the Commercial Woods" during the 19th century.

The White Pine is popular as an ornamental, and, in addition, it grows rapidly. A grove of White Pines "whispers" in the slightest breeze and lays down a thick carpet of brown, aromatic needles. The smooth, light-brown cones of *P. strobus* are a favorite food of the White-winged Crossbill, *Loxia leucoptera.*

In silhouette, the young White Pine is fully-shaped with upward-growing branches; in old age, it achieves a broad head, often irregular in form due to lost branches. It can grow as high as 150 feet. Long transplanted in England, it is known there as the Weymouth Pine (see preface).

The wood is nearly white, only faintly tinged with yellow; is soft, smooth, and seemingly grainless, yet strong. Easily worked and durable, it is a cabinetmaker's delight. *P. strobus* has two especially well-known varieties, *P. strobus* var. *glauca,* the Blue White Pine, and *P. strobus* var. *pendula,* the Weeping White Pine.

KEY

Strobus

Needles:	5 to a sheath; 2-5″ long; deciduous every 3 years; soft and flexible, bluish-green, often long with a fine white longitudinal line on the inner surfaces; basal sheath ⅝″ long with hair tufts below the insertion of the needles.
Cones:	Yellow-ochre to dark brown; 4-6″ long and smooth, without prickles; often curved on stalks up to 1″; seeds ¼″ long, oval, reddish-brown mottled with black, with 1″ long wing.
Branches:	Greenish or light-brown; ascending in youth, descending or horizontal in age.
Bark:	Thin and smooth in youth, rugose and fissured in age.
Introduced:	1705

PINUS STROBUS *Eastern White Pine*

PINUS TAEDA
Loblolly Pine

This fragrant and hardy pine is another of the "Big Four" timber trees of the American South and is one of the most plentiful pines in that area of the United States. "Loblolly" to southerners, it is also known as "Frankincense Pine" for its perfumed resin and high turpentine content and, also, the "Oldfield Pine," because of its vigor in oeing able to quickly spread over impoverished land. (There is, by way of relationship an "Old-field Mouse," *Peromyscus polionotus,* which occupies among small mammals the same niche as *P. Taeda* does among pines; each "takes over" where less hardy species falter and perish.)

The tree grows to from 90-100 feet high but the wood of the Loblolly is less robust and distinctly inferior to the other "Big-Four" yellow-woods, but, still, it is of tremendous commercial importance and is decidedly useful in boatbuilding, general carpentry and as a source for paper pulp. Although a "southern pine" it is more hardy than the others in its group and will grow as far north as New Jersey.

Many animals besides Old-field mice inhabit its vast, self-sown plantations, among which is the Fox Squirrel, *Sciurus niger.*

Loblolly was originally a seaman's term for "water gruel or spoon-meal." In the USA the name came to identify a mudhole . . . and in the South identified with trees growing in swamps. . . .

KEY

Needles: 3 to a sheath; 6-9″ long, bright-green, slightly twisted; margins minutely-toothed; median resin canals; sharp apex.

Cones: Oval-shaped, subterminal, 3-5″ long; light-brown with stout-based, reflexed prickle; seed, ¼″ long, dark brown mottled with black, ½″ wing.

Branches: Young shoots yellowish-brown, without down, and ridged; form a compact round top.

Bark: Reddish-brown with irregular fissures (nearly impossible to separate from other "Big-Four" trees).

 Loblolly

Introduced: 1713

58

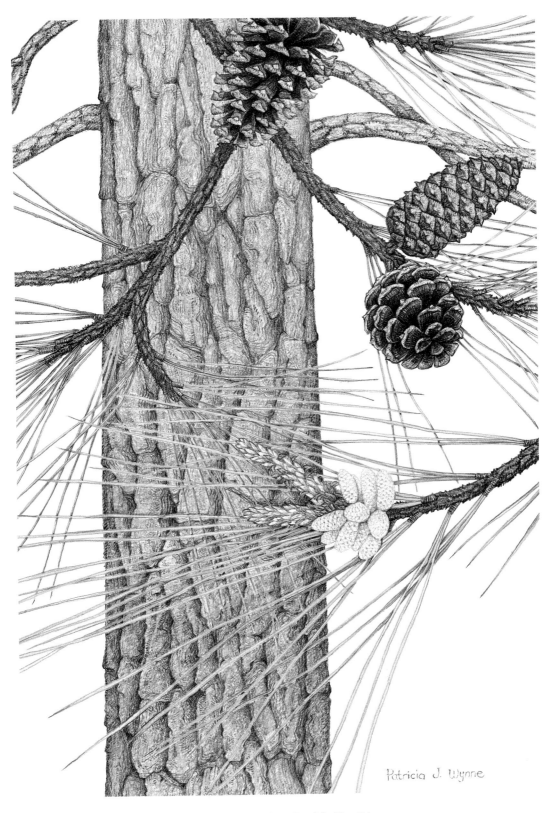

PINUS TAEDA *Loblolly Pine*

PINUS VIRGINIANA *Virginia Scrub Pine*

PINUS VIRGINIANA
Virginia Scrub Pine

This is the small, generally scraggly pine of the Pine Barrens of New Jersey. It is irregularly shped with greyish-green needles and a general appearance of bushy inelegance.

The wood of *P. virginiana* is decidely inferior and, except for fencing and firewood, or occasionally for railway sleepers or pulp, has little commercial value.

This tree, like *P. pungens,* is another type of scrub pine (only 30-40 feet high), which quickly takes over areas of poor soil, withal its less than satisfactory attributes. However, in the Shenandoah Valley, or in the Jersey Pine Barrens, amidst tea-colored streams flowing over white sands, close by to the native orchids, sundews and pitcher plants of the aromatic bogs, and in winter sheltering the little finch known as the Pine Siskin, *Spinus pinus,* as well as the Pine Grosbeak, *Pinicola enucleator,* this not overly attractive tree comes off looking better than it actually is.

KEY

virginiana

Needles: 2 to a sheath; 1¼-2½″ long, rigid, twisted, grey-green; irregular teeth, medium resin canals, sharp apex.

Cones: Abundant, always bent backwards on branches; oblong, 1-2½″ long, reddish-brown; with sharp prickle; seeds, small and pale brown and mottled, with wing only ¼″ long.

Branches: Distinguished from all other 2-leaved pines by its purplish shoots and waxy bloom.

Bark: Thin and scaly, grey-brown.

Introduced: before 1739

Other Eastern North American Pines

PINUS CLAUSA
Sand Pine

clausa

The Sand Pine is almost entirely contained within the state of Florida. It is another of the scrub pine group growing to a height of only 15-20′, and having timber unfit for any commercial purpose. This tree is able to prosper on the most meager of sandy soils but is of scarcely any value other than for fuel and as a sand-binder. Being another "scrub pine," it is closely allied to *P. virginiana*. It has two needles to a sheath and cones that are mainly in clusters and which remain closed on the branches, often for many years, before reluctantly releasing its seeds under the trauma of a severe forest fire.

PINUS ELLIOTTII
Slash Pine

slash →
elliottii

The Slash Pine is a coastal and low-altitude pine from southern South Carolina, south Georgia, and northern Florida. It is a large, tall tree of up to 100′ in height and is widely used commercially as a source of turpentine and rosin. The wood is of good quality and is often used as flooring. Needles are 2-3 to a sheath and crowded on the ends of the branches, slightly glossy and dark green, and are 7-10″ long. Cones are 2½-5″ long; tan or light-brown, and ending in a stout, grey prickle. Seeds are ovoid and somewhat three-angled, black or mottled grey, and with a well-developed wing. Bark is at first greyish, but with age becomes orange or orange-brown and sheds in large, flat, broad plates.

PINUS GLABRA
Spruce Pine

The Spruce Pine occupies the same geographical range as *P. elliottii*, the Slash Pine, i.e., from southern South Carolina through Georgia and northern Florida. It is a tree of neotropical, moist soils and humid atmosphere, and is nowhere abundant. The wood is very similar in appearance and strength to *P. taeda*, the Loblolly Pine, each being valuable for general carpentry and boatbuilding. However, the relative scarcity of *P. glabra* makes it of far less importance than the former. The needles are 2 to a stalk; soft, slender and twisted; medium-green and 1½ to 3" long. The cones are symmetrical, tawny-brown, and between 1¼ to 2" long on short stalks; they are soft with a weak prickle. The seeds are rough and triangular, $^3/_{16}$" long with a ½" wing.

glabra
Ceder pine

PINUS SEROTINA
Pond Pine

Pinus serotina is so closely related to *P. rigida*, the northern Pitch Pine, that many botanists consider the former to be simply a southern variety. However, it would seem to be validly distinguished from *P. rigida* by its much longer needles 6-8", by its longer sheaths, and by its more resinous winter buds. It grows in damp sand or wet, peaty soil.

PINUS ARISTATA
Bristlecone Pine

Western North American Pines

PINUS ARISTATA
Bristlecone Pine

"The world's oldest known living thing is a Bristlecone Pine," is a much-quoted statement, and no doubt true. An individual tree (*P. longaeva,* a newly described species—1970— formerly grouped under *P. aristata*) in the White Mountains of California, is known to be more than 4600 years old.

Forests comprised of this tree once covered large areas of the western United States, but in recent centuries its vitality has been sapped and it is senescent at best, lingering now in only isolated and remote areas of high altitude (7,000 to 12,000 feet). It is a dying species, in need of preservation, now found in a native state only in Colorado, eastern California, Nevada and Utah, and in small areas of Arizona and New Mexico.

The Bristlecone is generally twisted and contorted in form, and kept low in its habitat by conditions of adverse weather nd high winds. Its gnarled trunk, however, is often three to six feet in girth. When planted in the eastern United States or in England the pine is nearly always a dwarf.

Identifying this tree in a natural setting is simplified by its habitat: high from 7,000 to 12,000 feet. At that elevation it can be confused with *P. balfoùriana,* the Foxtail Pine, from which it differs in shape and size of the cones and the lack in *P. balfouriana* of the resinous exudations on the needles. At its lower elevations either tree can serve as home for the ubiquitous White-footed Mouse, *Peromyseus maniculatus.*

It was long thought that "the oldest tree in the world" might be one of the Giant Sequoias or, perhaps, one of the lesser-known rain forest giants, or even an Atlas Cedar. But careful research over a period of twenty years—a process of exhaustive coring and ring-width evaluation—led dendrochronologists to an arid area of California high in the Sierra Nevada range. There, in the White Mountains region, within the boundaries of the Inyo National Forest, they found a relatively large grove of these ancient trees. Windblasted, splintered, and generally scourged by the bitter adversity of that dry, hostile clime, many of the trees continue to survive, even though their trunks are little more than twisted stumps, scarcely 10–20 feet high, and their living parts are reduced to only a perimetric layer just under the bark. Still, however, seeds continue to grow to seedlings, and seedlings to saplings; but not within our lifetime. A single, slender stem may show as many as several hundred annual growth rings, so slow-growing are these trees.

The *National Geographic Magazine* of March 1958 contains an engrossing article by Dr. Edmund Schulman, a well-known dendrochronologist, that most vividly chronicles the story of *Pinus aristata* and its place in nature's realm.

KEY

aristata
Bristlecone

Needles: 5 to a sheath; incurved, 1½″, deciduous only every 14-17 years; densely-crowded; white-lined on inner surface, shining deep green on outer; marginal resin ducts; speckled with tiny white flecks of resin.

Cones: 3-3½″ long; sharp transverse spines with sharp prickle; light-brown, mottled with black; seed ⅓″ long with 1″ wing.

Branches: Young shoots sturdy, yellowish-brown, with tiny reddish-brown hairs.

Bark: Smooth, greenish-white, becoming scaly, contorted, and deeply ridged longitudinally with age.

Introduced: 1861

PINUS BALFOURIANA
Foxtail Pine

Confined to the high mountains of California, the Foxtail Pine is found in two distinct locations, one in the southern Sierras and the other in the Northern Coast Range. It is strictly an alpine species inured to the perpetual winds and frigid blasts of an artic clime.

Reaching a maximum height of 90 feet, but far more often seen at less than 50 feet, the Foxtail Pine is of virtually no commercial value even on a very local level; its habitat being generally too high and remote for even its occasional use as firewood. It is interesting, however, that the two basic populations—the one southern and mountain-bound and the other northern coastal—although looking much the same, differ vastly in the chemical compositions of their turpentines.

The Foxtail Pine is similar to the Bristlecone Pine but overreaches it in height and lacks the resinous droplets typical of *P. aristata,* and, even more obviously, it lacks the sharp stiletto of the cones of the latter and has instead only a minute incurved prickle on the cone plates.

Altogether, considering its general inaccessability and the light, soft, brittle nature of its wood, the Foxtail Pine serves little practical purpose for man.

KEY

Needles: 5 to a sheath; stout, coarse, sharp, and incurved; 1-1½″ long; deciduous 10-12 years; dark green with conspicuous white ventral stripe; pressed close to branches; lacks resinous droplets of *P. aristata.*

Cones: Sub-terminal, semi-round; dark purplish-brown; 3½-5″ long; scale-end flattened and with only small incurved prickle; seeds ⅓″ with 1″ wing.

Branches: Thin and smooth, minutely downy, whitish on young trees, darker on older trees.

Bark: Dark, red-brown with deep ridges covered with scales.

Introduced: 1852

balfouriana / Fox Tail

PINUS CONTORTA
Lodgepole Pine

Here again we have a conflict in vernacular meaning: "Lodgepole" would indicate that American Indians used this pine for the center-pole of their huts. They did, indeed. But why? Because it was, in effect, next door. Actually, this pine is most susceptible to what are called "favorable conditions of growth," and it varies from lodgepole saplings of reasonably linear form to what really borders on the grotesque: bent, gnarled, wind-tortured, rugose and dwarf. It is appropriately named *contorta* because of its twisted branches.

P. contorta is a tree "varying greatly in stature and habitat." Descriptions range from "a stunted tree" to a tree "200 feet high!" It would seem a difficult task to sensibly go about identifying or even taking seriously such a range of irrational description. In addition, we are asked to believe it is often called the Beach Pine when its range is to 3,350 meters—which is over 10,000 feet—in elevation.

But you must not blame the tree—nor the botanists. Whenever a tree, i.e., an "entity," a true and proper species, by its nature, spreads itself over varied geographical zones, it simply must change to meet the conditions wherein its seeds fall, rise and prosper. And so *P. contorta* is a hardy type of pine, vigorous and staunch, that ranges from Alaska to Baja California and from sea level to 10,000 feet over the major mountain ranges. As to "what it looks like," one must consider where one is.

All of the "contortions" we go through here, however, are our own. It—the pine itself—has the same chromosomes, cells, and physical structure, no matter where its seeds have randomly pronounced its distribution. On the Pacific strands its paired needles and light, yellowish-brown cones fall under the shadows of gulls' and terns' wings; in the High Sierras or the Rocky Mountains the same kinds of needles and cones—containing the selfsame chromosomes—will feel the weight of the elusive and ultra-feral Pine Marten, *Martens americana*, scurrying amidst their supportive branches.

This is another of the tightly-sealed cone trees that seldom open and disperse their seeds until they feel the heat of a forest fire.

The mountain variety is sometimes broken down into a botanical variety; *P. contorta* var. *latifolia,* and sometimes it is not. It is agreed, however, that this is "the commonest

PINUS CONTORTA   *Lodgepole Pine*

coniferous tree of the northern Rocky Mountains and of the Black Hills [South Dakota] and extends to large forests.'' At this rate, little wonder the Indians used it for teepee-poles and varied supports. There was little else around.

This pine is often of slow growth, with close annual rings. Although the coastal trees of this species are relatively worthless in timber value, the true ''Lodgepole'' of the high mountain areas is suitable for lumber usage even with its manifold knots. At its best it is relatively straight-grained and moderately strong, useful for such applications as building interiors, boat-building, and general construction.

Generally, this tree is intolerant of shade and grows at its best on dry, gravelly soil. In exposed areas where its seeds have sprouted amongst rocky outcroppings, the normally tall lodgepole-type, *P. contorta* var. *latifolia,* will become stunted and closely resemble the dwarfed, coastal variety of *contorta* (nominally, then, the specific type—but, of course, in that form, contradicting the popular English designation of ''Lodgepole'').

KEY

Lodgepole

Needles: 2 to a sheath; persisting 3-8 years; yellowish-green, often of a metallic luster; twisted, varying from 1-3″ long to ⅛″ wide; not easily distinguishable, rudimentary teeth; ending in blunt point; basal sheath to ⅛-¼″ long.

Cones: Sub-terminal, solitary or in pairs or clusters; 1-2″, opening when ripe or remaining closed for years, then opening; short stalks; ovoid or conical; light lustrous, yellow-brown, with a small, decidedly down-curved often deciduous, prickle; seeds long, $⅛-\frac{1}{6}″$, reddish-brown with dark spots.

Branches: Young shoots green, without down, becoming brown in second year.

Bark: Reddish-brown, ¼-¾″ thick, dividing into thin scales.

Introduced: 1855

PINUS COULTERI
Big-cone Pine

The coastal ranges of California from San Francisco south to Baja and the Mexican border are the home of this most unique pine. "Big-cone?" To say "big" means nothing except as a means of comparison when referring to cones—but big is the only applicable word when one considers that these cones are something the size of a football: 10 to 14 inches long by 6 inches wide, the heaviest cones borne by any of the pines.

Cones of such a bizarre size are a curiosity—especially to visitors to California—and cones-for-mantels-, guilded cones, painted cones, cone-lamps, and an endless array of other cone-products have long been a local item of trade in the counties where this pine is commonly found.

Not much else is needed by way of identification but *P. coulteri* is diploxylon and it is interesting to note that it is closely related to *P. sabiniana,* the Digger Pine, of the dry foothills of the California Central Valley, and the rare *P. torreyana* from San Diego (Del Mar) and Santa Rosa Island. These coarse, straggly, sparsely-fed types of pines give a hint to the structure and habitat of *P. coulteri,* and just, perhaps—from a nonscientific point of view—some clue as to the reason for the big cones. In such arid and hostile habitat, perhaps a large and sturdy seed is the answer to survival.

At its best—presumably by way of nourishment—this tree can reach a height of 80 feet, but the general range is much lower, 30 feet being generous enough by way of latitude. It is a pine of the dry mountain slopes of lower California, occurring singly or in only small groups at elevations of from 3,000 to 7,000 feet.

The wood is weak and brittle with exceptionally large resin ducts and has little value besides local use as fuel. The seeds (reminiscent again of the arid-land piñon pines) are edible.

P. coulteri makes a very interesting ornamental and garden tree, not only because of its large cones, but because its branches have the poetic habit of wide-branching and conical aspect.

This pine was named in honor of Thomas Coulter, the Irish botanist, who collected extensively in California and Mexico, and died in 1843.

PINUS COULTERI *Big-cone Pine*

Needles: 3 to a sheath; dark, bluish-green; deciduous every 2-3 years; very thick, in clusters, very stiff, curved, stoutly-proportioned, 6-12″ long; toothed margins; resin canals medial or marginal (variable); basal sheath 1½″ long.

Cones: Large and massive, weighing 2-5 pounds; when green, oblong ovoid, 10-14″ long, 6″ wide; scales thick, woody, 2½″ long, 1½″ wide; curved hook or claw, rather than "prickle"; seed large, oval, 1½″ long with 1″ wing, edible.

Branches: The buds are large, stout and resinous. Young shoots yellowish-green, are stout, smooth, without down, prominently ridged, and become orange-brown with age.

Bark: Thick, dark brown; deeply and irregularly fissured.

Introduced: 1832

coulteri

PINUS FLEXILIS
Limber Pine

Certain pines are noted for their "inflexibility," i.e., their disinclination, in a feral state, to cross with other species. *P. flexilis* is not one of these; it has four firmly established varieties at the moment and, given other opportunities of natural transplantation, it may well come up with yet another or more. *Flexilis* means pliant or limber.

The Limber Pine is an alpine species of only medium height, 20-60 feet, and most commonly found on the eastern slopes of the Rocky Mountains from Canada to Texas, and east to Sioux City, Nebraska, although stands exist in Arizona and southern California. Because it is found only at higher elevations, generally away from commercial access, it is not a timber tree, as such, although its wood is soft and of fair quality and is easily worked. It is only used locally for any practical purpose.

A symbiotic relationship is shared between *P. flexilis* and the White Pine Butterfly, *Neopharis menapita,* which lives upon and spends its entire life span on or near this tree.

KEY

Needles: 5 to a sheath, deciduous 5-6 years; medium green; 2-3″ long, pointing forward, rigid and densely packed, curved or slightly twisted; marginal resin canals.

Cones: No stalks, ovoid; erect in youth, spreading when mature; 3-5″ long; orange or buff in color; see reddish-brown, mottled with dark brown, ½″ long with insignificant wing, shed as soon as ripened.

Branches: Young shoots without down and with fine brownish hairs; young branches smooth.

Bark: Dark brown, 1″ thick and fissured in ridges.

Introduced: 1861

flexilis

74

PINUS FLEXILIS
Limber Pine

PINUS JEFFREYI *Jeffrey Pine*

PINUS JEFFREYI
Jeffrey Pine

The Jeffrey Pine is essentially a California pine although it does extend into southern Oregon, into western Nevada and as far south as Baja California. It is very close in appearance to the Ponderosa Pine (and is also tall—to 190 feet), except in having brighter needles and bark, the bark being usually cinnamon-red rather than *P. ponderosa*'s dark brown. But there are also microscopic as well as chemical differences: for example, *P. ponderosa* contains terpenes but no heptane, while *P. jeffreyi* contains no terpenes but does have heptanes—therefore the crushed stems of *P. ponderosa* have the odor of turpentine, while those of *P. jeffreyi* have the fragrance of pineapple.

The wood is much like that of *P. ponderosa,* a good timber tree of the hard-pine variety, and the tree has value as an ornamental but only on the West Coast.

Many interesting birds and mammals inhabit the Pacific coastal mountains but one is among the unique: *Phenocomys longicardus*, the Red Tree Mouse, lives among the misty crowns of the Douglas Firs and Jeffrey Pines, and some—particularly the females—are born and die in the tops of these trees and never even touch the ground. These mice feed on the needles and bark of these conifers and drink only dew and rainwater.

Jeffreyi

KEY

Needles:	3 to a sheath; 5-15″ long, bluish-green (*P. ponderosa* is dark green); rigid; straighter needles; toothed margins; sharp apex, stoma on each surface; basal sheath ⅞″ long.
Cones:	Ovoid-oblong; 5-12″; curved prickles; short-stalked; sub-terminal; light, reddish-brown; seeds, ½″ long with large wing.
Branches:	Spreading, drooping—but ascending at tips.
Bark:	Cinnamon-red with large and thick plates looking much like parts of a puzzle.
Introduced:	1853

windblown Jeffrey

77

PINUS LAMBERTIANA
Sugar Pine

The Sugar Pine of Oregon and California is the "Giant Red-wood" of its genus: the largest and tallest of all the pines in the world, attaining a height of 250 feet or more with a girth of more than 40 feet. It has a straight trunk that is often clear of branches for over 100 feet from the ground.

The name "Sugar Pine" comes from a sugary exuda-tion from the once-cut heartwood. Natives to the area claim the usual medicinal properties that local people attach to nearly any growing thing—in this case a catharsis—but, in actuality, the sap accumulations do have a sweet base and have been used as a sugar substitute and even for a "pine candy." The seeds, also, are eaten, but it is said that they are inferior in quality to other pine seeds.

The tree is one of the most prominent species on the western slope of the Sierra Nevada Mountains from 2,000 to 9,000 feet. But in many places where it thrives, because it does not produce cones with any degree of regularity, it is being encroached upon by the ubiquitous and persistnt *P. ponderosa*.

The wood is of first-class quality, soft, straight-grained and strong; and only slightly inferior to that of the Eastern White Pine, *P. strobus*. It is particularly noted for its availabil-ity in boards of large size without knothole or other blemishes.

P. lambertiana was named for Aylmer Bourke Lam-bert (1761-1842), author of *The Genus Pinus* (1804), by David Douglas (1798-1834).

KEY

Sugar

Needles:	5 to a sheath; deciduous every 3 years; 3½-4" long, sharp, rigid, twisted; dark blue-green; finely toothed margins; stomata on both sides; basal sheath ¾" long.
Cones:	Sub-terminal; 12-24" long, 3-4" wide, medium-brown; no prickle; erect and purple when young, pendulous with age; with ¾" long stalks and borne on top-most branches; seed ½" long, with 1½" wing; shed when ripe.
Branches:	Young shoots completely covered with fine down; smooth in youth.
Bark:	2-3" thick; with irregular, scaly ridges; cinnamon-red.
Introduced:	1827

PINUS LAMBERTIANA   *Sugar Pine*

PINUS MONTICOLA   *Western White Pine*

PINUS MONTICOLA
Western White Pine

This is another of the gigantic pines of the Pacific coastal mountain ranges reaching an elevation of 10,000 feet, and is often found associated with the Sugar Pine, *P. Lambertiana*.

P. monticola is the western counterpart of the Eastern White Pine, *P. strobus*, but larger and even more robust, attaining a height of over 200 feet. Again, unlike its eastern cousin, *P. monticola* is generally recognized by its conical form, by its bark being distinctly divided into squarish plates on the older trees, by its stouter needles and more downy shoots.

The wood of this tree is very like *P. strobus* except that it is perhaps coarser. Certainly it is a fine, clear wood, relatively resin-free and as easily worked and as valuable for cabinetry as the eastern wood.

This great tree, which seldom has fertile cones before 40-60 years, is often host to the Williamson's Sapsucker, *Sphyrapicus thyroidens*, a rather bizarre woodpecker-like bird from the high mountains of the west. Its name, *monticola*, refers to its preference for mountainous areas.

KEY

Needles: 5 to a sheath; deciduous 3-4 years; soft, bluish-green in color; more rigid and more stout than *P. strobus;* 2-4" long; densely-packed on branches; with fine but distinct teeth on margins; stomata in multiple lines, inner surface only; marginal resin canals; basal sheath ¾" long.

Cones: Solitary or in clusters; slender and pendulous; green or purple in color 5-8" long; short and stout stalks; no prickles; seeds, reddish-brown with black spots, and small, wings 1" long, and shed as soon as ripe.

Branches: Stout young shoots, covered with reddish down; young branches light grey, thin and smooth.

Bark: Greyish-brown on older trees, separated into squarish plates.

Introduced: 1851

monticola

PINUS PONDEROSA
Ponderosa Pine

Pinus ponderosa is a typically massive timber pine of the mountains and mesa country of the American west; it is also well-known as the Western Yellow Pine and is the most widely distributed species in western North America, with the exception of the Sugar Pine, *P. lambertiana*. It covers vast areas from British Columbia south to Mexico and from the Pacific Ocean eastward to Nebraska and Texas.

It is a tall tree—from 100 to 200 feet (usually ranging between 100 to 150 feet)—with a long, clean expanse of trunk before spreading out into stout and often pendulous branches.

The wood of *P. ponderosa* is hard, strong, close-grained, and firm, with conspicuous resin ducts. It is not durable in contact with the soil, unless treated. Usually, it is used in heavy construction and general carpentry.

Basically, although stately and handsome, the Ponderosa Pine is a heavy-timber tree, a "crop," and it is annually havested as such and replanted for its commercial value. Many animals, birds included, use the tall Ponderosa as stairways and food-bins, but one of the strangest is a rare and local animal found only in the Ponderosa stands along the 40 to 50 mile island forest on the north rim of the Grand Canyon—the Kaibab Squirrel, *Sciurnus kaibabensis*, whose beautiful pelage and long ear tufts show the effect of isolation on species that are confined to inaccessible habitats.

P. ponderosa is highly susceptible to predations of, in particular, the barkbeetle *Dendroctonus brevicomis*, other bark beetles, certain parasitic fungi, and a variety of mistletoes that cause Ponderosa branches to be stunted and unhealthy.

KEY

Needles: 3 to a sheath; dark, or yellowish-green (depending on the location); deciduous 3-4 years; spreading and densely-crowded on branches; rigid, 5-10″ long, curved, with minutely-toothed margins; stomatic lines on each surface, median resin canals; basal sheath ⅞″ long.

Cones: Solitary or in clusters, sub-terminal, without stalks; ovoid, 3-10″ long, 2½-4½″ wide; light, reddish-brown; often, when falling, leaving a few basal scales attached to branches; apex of scales with a minute prickle; seed oval, ¼″ long, mottled, with ¾″ wing.

Branches: Stout, spreading, often-drooping—but ascending at the tips; young shoots, green or orange-brown at first, but becoming nearly black.

Bark: Yellowish, or dark, reddish-brown; with irregularly scaly plates becoming thick in mature trees.

Introduced: 1827 (First reported in 1804 by the Lewis & Clark Expedition; named by David Douglas in 1826)

ponderosa

PINUS PONDEROSA
Ponderosa Pine

Other Western North American Pines
Haploxylon Pines

PINUS ALBICAULIS
White-bark Pine

albicaulis

A subalpine tree that grows as high as 5,000 to 12,000 feet—ranging from British Columbia to Mexico and east through the Rocky Mountains to Wyoming. *P. albicaulis* has a contorted trunk and twisted branches and is of little practical use. In a way, it vaguely resembles the Lace-bark Pine of the Orient in that the bark of young trees is whitish and smooth, and in the older tree the bark is thin and scales off in small patches. The needles occur 5 to a sheath; similar to *P. flexilis*. Cones are dark purple in youth, lighter brown when mature; 1½-3″; thickened scales; sharp prickle; ½″ long, small wing; seeds do not shed when ripe. The branches are contorted and irregular, and the bark is whitish and smooth in youth; in age thin and scaling.

PINUS EDULIS
Two-leaved Nut Pine; Colorado Piñon

pinyon seed
(pine nut)
usually var.
edulis

Another of the edible-nut pines, *P. edulis* has only two leaves to a sheath. It ranges more eastward than others of its kind (piñon group) extending as far as western Oklahoma. Growing on arid mesas, it is generally a medium-sized, spreading tree of little commercial value.

PINUS MONOPHYLLA
Single-leaf Pine

monophylla
needles
2½″

Significant in having only one needle to a sheath which gives it an odd, "spikey" look, this pine tree grows in Nevada, Utah, and northern Arizona. Mostly a desert species, it is yet another edible-nut piñon pine, low and scrublike as are others of its kind.

PINUS ATTENUATA
Knob-cone Pine

The Knob-cone pine is a small tree, only 20 to 50 feet high, and chiefly grows in the California area but extends to some degree northward to Oregon and south to Baja California. It grows at altitudes of 1,800 feet in the northern growths but to 4,000 feet in California. Straight and well-formed trunks may reach 75 feet in height but in low elevations of California are scrubby, forked and low—equally, this tree is drought resistant. The needles are 3 to a sheath, grey-green and slender, 4-7″. The tawny-yellow cones from which this pine derives its name, are like a child's crooked top, 3-5″, and most often asymmetrical at the base; they generally appear in clusters. The ¼″ seed is oval, long and black with 1″ long wing.

attenuata cone 4-5″

PINUS MURICATA
Obispo Pine; Prickle-cone Pine

A strictly coastal California pine ranging onto Santa Cruz and neighboring islands, growing on rocky, maritime headlands. It has been proposed that *P. muricata* be divided into four varieties. This pine grows from sea level to an altitude of about 900 feet. It is rarely more than 50-60′ high and has crooked, irregular branches that form an uneven, flat-topped crown with dense, dark-green foliage. The wood is of moderate quality but is only used locally for it is not plentiful enough for export. The unusually dark needles occur 2 to a sheath, are crowded, stiff, and curved with a slight twist. The cones are solitary or in small clusters, 2-3″ long; the scales are very hard, swollen at the apex, and terminate in a vicious, sharp prickle. The cones often persist on the tree for *30-40 years* before being liberated by forest fires when they then often form a thick ground cover.

PINUS RADIATA
Monterey Pine

Namesake of its environment—coastal California in the Monterey Peninsula where its range is restricted to a very small area of hilly ground near the sea—this popular pine has a uniquely limited range but is successful in plantings in the southern hemisphere; for example, it is an important timber tree in New Zealand. It crosses in nature with *P. attenuata*. It is tall and well-formed with thick, dark-brown trunks in open-growth. It survives and propogates well at sea level in range of salt spray. Contorted by environmental conditions, this pine has a "Japanese-style" of graceful irregularity, much-beloved by its human neighbors. Its 3 to-a-sheath needles are a cheerful, bright green and are long and slender. The cones are large, greyish-brown and glossy. The seeds are ellipsoid and blackish.

radiata
   tree & cone
ᴍONTEREY

PINUS SABINIANA
Digger Pine

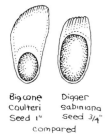

Big cone   Digger
Coulteri   sabiniana
Seed 1"   Seed 3/4"
   compared

Also, strictly California, this pine thrives among the foothills of the mountains of this state's Central Valley. It has slender, lacy grey-green foliage which in age is "scraggly" and rises to 40-80' in height. Its growth range has shrunk rather drastically due to timbering and destruction by man (Mirov). Like *P. coulteri,* the cone of which is the size of a football, this pine also has one of the most enormous cones of all pines (although still not to the size of *P. coulteri*) 8-10" long and 4" wide at the base and has a huge talonlike hook of a prickle. A curious difference, however, is that although the cone itself is smaller than *P. coulteri,* the seed is even larger (see sketch) although it has a smaller wing. The wood is weak and brittle and inconsequential. The large, edible seeds once formed a major part of the diet of the Digger Indians from which tribe this pine is named.

PINUS TORREYANA
Torrey Pine

Yet another Tertiary relic, this small, stout-branched tree is found near the Del Mar Peninsula and Santa Rosa Island in California. Low and crooked now it was a fairly stately tree in ages past. It does well in cultivation where it assumes a candelabralike form with heavy branches. Widespread from Tertiary through Oligocene and Miocene periods, this tree now seems to be a dying species. The dark green needles occur 5 to a sheath and are arranged in heavy tufts on the branches, and are 7-10″ long. The cones are broadly ovoid, dark brown, 4-5½″ long, and the same in width at the base. Seeds are ellipsoid, dull brown and mottled and are sweet, oily, and edible. The wood is of poor quality but the seeds have long been used as a food. This tree is also called the Soledad pine.

torreyana

torreyana
seedling
(no stem!)

     This tree was named for John Torrey, American botanist, 1796-1873. Torrey was from New York City.

PINUS WASHOENSIS
Washoe Pine

So recently discovered (only in 1938) this pine still does not have a descriptive common (vernacular) name, but honors the Washoe Indians who used to hunt east of Lake Tahoe where it is found. *P. washoensis* apparently flourished in its native state but was timbered heavily during the development of Nevada's silver mines. It looks like *P. ponderosa* but its cones resemble *P. jeffreyi*. It intermingles with *P. jeffreyi* but "does not appear to hybridize at present" (1959). In nearly every way this tree resembles *P. jeffreyi,* except in its obviously smaller cones, only 2-3″ long, and rather smaller needles, 4-6″ long. There are also "other less obvious differences in structure, biochemistry, and behavior" (Mirov), which may prove to be even more significant as more refinements in these specializations are explored and utilized.

PINUS AYACAHUITE
Mexican White Pine

Patricia J. Wynne

Mexican Pines

PINUS AYACAHUITE
Mexican White Pine

Pinus ayacahuite is very much a Mexican pine, extending north only to the very border of the United States. It has the graceful flow in silhouette of the Himalayan White Pine, *P. Wallichiana*. The Mexican White Pine is found on mountain slopes and at the head of ravines in Central America north into all of Mexico. Of course, being a White Pine, it is a haploxylon or "soft" pine, with physical properties of the wood being in the better range of quality. The tree can be quite high—up to 150 feet—but is generally 90-100 feet.

The Mexican White Pine has two recognized varieties, *P. ayacahuite* var. *brachyptera*, that differs in having an abnormally large seed with a very short and inadequate wing; and *P. ayacahuite* var. *veitchii*, that has larger cones, larger seeds with, again, shorter wings.

KEY

Needles: 5 to a sheath; slender and spreading from the sheath; 4-8″ long; bluish-green; deciduous every 3 years; finely-toothed margins; flat inner surface with 3-4 lines of stomata; deciduous basal sheath.

Cones: Sub-terminal, large—8-18″ long; 2½-6″ wide; cylindrical but tapering at apex; on stalks 1-2″ long; enlarged tips often resinous; seed small, ⅜″ long with well-developed wing, grey-brown mottled with dark brown.

Branches: Young shoots covered with soft orange-colored hairs; branchlets yellowish-brown; slender, spreading branches.

Bark: Thin and smooth, except becoming scaly in age and fissured; brownish-grey.

Introduced: 1840

ayacahuite

89

PINUS CEMBROIDES
Piñon Pine

Patricia J. Wynne

PINUS CEMBROIDES
Piñon Pine (here shown)

All piñon pines are haploxylon and all, to a great degree, resemble *P. cembroides*. (Since this book is limited to practical field study, it would be a redundancy to expand on each of the seven species, as do certain of the definitive works listed in the Appendix).

In essence, they are all Mexican, but overflowing north into the southwestern United States and, south, into some Central American countries bordering Mexico; they are all "edible-nut" pines; and they all, if not small and scrubby trees, are certainly never tall or imposing.

P. cembroides is often called the "Mexican Nut Pine;" "piñon" is simply the Spanish word for "pine nut." It is seen mostly as a bushy or low-growing tree, seldom more than 20 feet high, with a short trunk and rounded top. For centuries, the Indians of the southwestern United States gathered its nuts as did birds, squirrels, and now, tourists.

The Piñon Pine grows in open stands—closely-packed, with the look of cultivated orchards—on semi-arid tablelands in the Southwest and in Mexico. Many small birds and other animals have the nutritious Piñon seeds as a staple of their diets; but two, in particular, are actually named for their symbiotic connection with these trees: namely, the Piñon Jay, *Gymnorhinnus cyanocephala*, an odd jay, in habit more like a small, blue crow; and the Piñon Mouse, *Peromyscus truei*, a white-footed mouse with extremely large ears.

The wood of the Piñon Pine is moderately heavy for pine. It is slow-growing, often knotty, and although used locally for building purposes, mine timber, fencing, and firewood, is hardly a marketable item of any consequence.

Note: *P. monophylla, P. edulis,* and *P. quadrifolia* as well as *P. pinceana, P. nelsonii,* and *P. culminicola* are regarded by many authors as varieties of *Pinus cembroides;* however, Mirov (1967) prefers their inclusion as species.

KEY

Needles:	3 to a sheath: deciduous every 3-4 years; closely-arranged, incurved, 1-2" long; sharply pointed; stomata on ventral surface; segments of leaf-sheath persisting; glaucous-green.
Cones:	Globose or egg-shaped, 1-1½" long; reddish-brown; scales few, large, flat, wide-spreading; seeds, ½-¾" long, ¼-⅜" wide, wingless, edible.
Branches:	Dark orange; at first, pubescent.
Bark:	Thin and scaly.
Introduced:	1830

cembroides

Other Mexican Pines
Haploxylon Pines

PINUS STROBIFORMUS
(No English Name)

Classified as Mexican (northern) but ranges into Arizona, New Mexico, Utah and Colorado. Very little apparently is known of this pine. It is a five-needled "White Pine" type of tree.

Strobus

PINUS STROBUS VAR. CHIAPENSIS
Chiapes Pine

Described in 1940 as a variety separate from the Eastern *strobus* pine, the cones are quite similar. The range is doubtful but it grows to altitudes of 6,000 feet. It is found on coffee and banana plantations at elevations to 3,600 feet. It forms forests in Guatemala. Currently only native to Mexico there may be some cross-breeding.

Diploxylon Pines

PINUS ARIZONICA
Arizona Pine

Once considered a variety of *P. ponderosa*, this pine has been isolated into a separate species (see below for range). This tree is very straight and very tall and is rapidly being exploited for timber.

PINUS CHIHUAHUANA
Chihuahua Pine

A 3-needle Mexican species native to Chihuahua, Sonora and Durango and northward into southern reaches of Arizona and New Mexico. Has been recorded at 7,500 feet altitude. Often regarded as a variety of *P. leiophylla,* but would seem to have stouter, more rigid needles.

PINUS COOPERII
Cooper's Pine

A new species (1940) this pine is called "pino amarillo"—yellow pine—and is strictly a Mexican species. As are many others, this pine is very close to *P. montezumae.*

PINUS DOUGLASIANA
(No English Name)

Needles soft and thick—named for Margeret Douglas, a North American, who greatly admired Mexican flora and wished to protect it. This pine grows best at elevations of 4,500 to 7,000 feet.

PINUS DURANGENSIS
Durango Pine

"El pino real"—6,7,8 needles in sheath—confined to Mexico's Durango-Sierra Madre range. A *P. montezumae* type tree.

PINUS ENGELMANII
Apache Pine

engelmannii/APACHE CONE 4-6"

This pine is closely allied to *P. ponderosa* from which it differs in having much longer needles 10-16" long, in groups of 3, 4 or 5. Its turpentine lacks turpene, delta-3-carene, which is found in *P. ponderosa*. It is native to the extreme southwestern U.S. and Mexico.

PINUS GREGGII
Gregg's Pine

Limited strictly to northeastern Mexico this pine is similar to *P. patula* but coarser and with short needles that are erect rather than drooping, and by the smooth grey bark on the upper trunk. Needles are 3 to a sheath, bright green, and slender. Cones are irregular and tawny-yellow.

PINUS HARTWEGII
Hartweg Pine

This pine is found near the line of permanent snow in the central mountains of Mexico. At Popocatepetl and Iztaccihuatl there are large "pure stands" of this pine. Needles are in bundles of 3-4, greyish-green. Cones are dark brown—nearly black—when mature.

PINUS HERRERAI
(No English Name)

A 3-needle pine, soft and flexible. Only discovered in 1939. Very rare. Found in the Mexican states of Jalisco and Durango to an elevation of 7,000 feet.

PINUS LAWSONII
Lawson's Pine

P. lawsonii is a subtropical pine of southern Mexico. It differs from *P. montezumae* chiefly in its glaucous-green foliage. It is a large tree 80-100' high, and has needles in bundles of 3, 4 or 5. The bark is dark grey and scaly.

PINUS LEIOPHYLLA
(No English Name)

P. leiophylla is confined to subtropical Mexico from Oaxaca to the northern border. It is a tree of moderate size. Needles in bundles of 5, short, 3-4" long, slender, grey-green. Cones are biennial, which distinguishes them from all allied species other than *P. montezumae*.

leiophylla - cone
chihuahuane - 1½"
(hard pine which
sheds its sheath!)

PINUS LUMHOLTZII
Lumholtz Pine

A beautiful and graceful pine with bright yellowish-green drooping needle clusters and "cinnamon-red sheaths". The needles are 8-12" long. Cones are dull brown and symmetrical; 2" long. *P. lumholtzii* is native to the western Sierra of Mexico.

PINUS MICHOACANA
(No English Name)

This is a little-known pine of central Mexico, with needles in bundles of 5, 10-17" long, drooping and bright green. Cones are ovoid and large, 10-12" long, 4-5" wide, brown turning to grey. The status of this species is questionable and in need of revision. It appears to be closely allied to *P. montezumae*.

PINUS MONTEZUMAE
Montezuma Pine

montezumae

The Montezuma Pine is a "mother-pine" in that it is, in itself, an established, but variable type, that has many varieties and other little-known pines which resemble it. The tree is well-named for the Aztec Montezuma whose name is said to mean "He who shoots arrows in all directions." Among the 5-needled pines, *P. montezumae* can be generally separated by its long, spreading, and drooping needle clusters. It is one of the most beautiful of pines, being thick, bluish-green, 10" long, "weeping" clusters of needles that sweep downward in graceful arcs. The cones are large to 10" long—varying in size and shapes, and varying from dull yellow to reddish, even to dark brown in color. The tree grows to a height of 70-100 feet in the mountains of Mexico at elevations from 4,000 to 12,000 feet.

PINUS OAXACANA
(No English Name)

Pinus oaxacana is a *P. montezumae*-type pine from the Mexican states of Oaxaca and adjacent states. It has 8-12" needles, 5 to a bundle, and 4-5" cones. It is reported to have a high proportion of heptone in its oleo-resin, which serves to differentiate it from *P. montezumae*.

PINUS OOCARPA
(No English Name)

This has been called "the most southerly pine of the "New World." *P. oocarpa* is native to much of Central America and north into Mexico, from sea level to 3,500 feet. It is a medium-sized tree—to 60 feet—with needles in bundles of 3, 4 or 5, 10-12" long, and bright green. The cones are broadly-ovoid and long-stalked, greyish- or greenish-yellow.

96

PINUS PATULA
Jelecote Pine

The Jelecote pine is also called "the spreading-leaved pine." Its needles are 3, 4 or 5 to a sheath, bright green, slender, 6-12" long, curved and oblique at the base, and are pale-brown and shining. It is a graceful tree 40-60' high, with a trunk that often forks at a short distance from the ground and having long, spreading branches. It is native to central and eastern Mexico.

PINUS PRINGLEI
Pringle Pine

The Pringle Pine is confined to the southwestern regions of Mexico. Needles are 3 to a sheath, slender, curving upward at the ends. Medium green. Cones are asymmetrical on stout stalks, 2-4" long. The bark is dark grey and scaly.

PINUS PSEUDOSTROBUS
False White Pine

Similar to and intercrosses and hybridizes with *P. montezumae* and has varied characteristics. Native apparently to San Salvador only.

PINUS RUDIS
(No English Name)

Another offshoot of *P. montezumae* with which it hybridizes, but it is often treated as a variety. Mexico south to Guatemala. Not northern—confined to southern Mexican states. Is found at elevation of 4,000 meters. Described as, "a handsome pine."

PINUS TENUIFOLIA
(No English Name)

Very little known. A White Pine akin to *P. pseudostrobus* and to *P. montezumae*.

PINUS TEOCOTE
Aztec Pine

Native to the Sierras of Mexico this tree grows from 30-90' high. Generally distinguished by its small cones. Needles range from 2 to 4, 5 to a sheath, 4-7" long, spreading, twisted, and rigid. Cones are ovoid-oblong, 2" long, dull brown.

Caribbean Pines
(No Haploxylon Pines) Diploxylon Pines

PINUS CARIBAEA
Caribbean Pine

caribaena

The Caribbean Pine is a tropical species found throughout the Caribbean chain of islands and in Guatemala, Nicaragua, and Honduras. However, it is so closely allied to *P. elliottii,* the southern Slash Pine, that except for a questionable variance in the number of needles per sheath (4-5 instead of 2-3), with less prominent prickles, and smaller, narrower seeds, it is virtually identical, except for its geographic range.

PINUS CUBENSIS
Cuban Pine

Very closely allied to *P. caribaea* except for long, slender needles (to 6" long) and except young cones. Mature cones are

2-3″ long, symmetrical, nut-brown, with a shallow, recurved prickle. Grows at elevations from 900-4,500 feet.

PINUS ELLIOTTII *var.* DENSA
Florida Slash Pine

Confined to extreme southern Florida, this variety of the Slash Pine varies from its specific form only in that, as stemless seedlings, they resemble tussocks of grass, and in that the wood would seem to be of better quality. Further, some experts even doubt its linkage to *P. elliottii* and place it with *P. caribaea*. Clearly this is a variety that yet remains open to controversy.

PINUS OCCIDENTALIS
Cuban (Haitian) Pine

Found almost entirely on the island of Hispaniola (i.e., the Dominican Republic and Haiti), *P. occidentalis* is practically identical to *P. cubensis* of eastern Cuba, except that in the Dominican Republic and in Haiti the tree ascends to 7,000-9,000 feet.

PINUS TROPICALIS
(No English Name)

This vaguely-defined pine—again, nearly identical to *P. occidentalis* and *P. cubensis*—grows only at sea level in western Cuba in gravelly or sandy conditions or in low, rolling terrain only slightly above sea level. Note: It would seem pertinent to suggest that, in the encompassment of Caribbean species, they would all appear to be quite similar to the Slash Pine of the American south, *P. elliottii,* and that their differentiation is more a matter for botanical refinement than to be given much consideration in a field guide.

PINUS CEMBRA *Swiss Stone Pine*

Mediterranean Pines

PINUS CEMBRA
Swiss Stone Pine

Cembra is an alpine village and *Pinus cembra* is a truly alpine pine—seldom found in its natural state below 5,000 fet, where it extends across Europe's Alps. In cultivation, it has become a standard hardy pine for ornamental planting, especially suited in formal settings.

The Swiss Stone Pine in nature is a tall tree—70 to sometimes 120 feet, with spreading but short branches forming a narrow, dense, sprucelike pyramid. In old age, however, it can become quite picturesque with a broad aspect and round-topped head. But *P. cembra* is much more than an ornamental prop: the wood is useful and easily worked, its branches make an aromatic bed or bower, and the seeds are quite delicious, and (under the pseudonym of "pine kernels") enhance the pastries of many peoples over the vast alpine backbone of Europe and Asia.

Note: *P. cembra* is different from all other five-leaved species, excepting *P. koraiensis* and *P. sibirica*, in having a distinctive orange-brown matting of hairs—often just a bloom or pubescence—on the young shoots. In *P. koraiensis* this tomentose condition is similar but the cones are very different, leaves are stouter, and the marginal teeth are numerous, extending to the apex. *P. sibirica* has larger cones, larger leaves, and its seeds have husks. Also, in *P. cembra*, the cones never open: the seeds are liberated only by the rotting of the conal scales or by being scattered by birds and other animals in search of food.

KEY

Needles: 5 to a sheath; 2-4″ long, straight, dorsally dark green, ventrally bluish-white; marginal teeth, but widely-spaced and not extending to apex; medial resin ducts; deciduous 3-5 years.

Cones: Sub-terminal and short-stalked; egg-shaped and erect, 2½-3½″; greenish with violet tinge in growth, purplish-brown when ripe; scales rounded in outline, minutely downy on surface; never opening; seeds wingless, ½″ long, creamy-white, germinating (when freed) only after second year, edible by humans.

Branches: Young shoots clothed with dense orange-colored down; winter buds long-pointed, narrow, and resinous, dull brown with white, membranous margins: in youth, branches greenish-grey and smooth.

Bark: Reddish-grey, divided into thin, scaly plates.

Introduced: 1875

cembra

101

PINUS PEUCE   *Balkan Pine or Macedonian Pine*

PINUS PEUCE
Balkan Pine or Macedonian Pine

This tree somewhat resembles the Swiss Stone Pine, *P. cembra,* of even higher elevations, being narrowly conical in outline and of limited distribution, confined to mountain areas in the Balkan peninsula in Albania, Bulgaria, Yugoslavia and Greece. The tree is slow-growing with short ascending branches, forming a compact pyramidal mass. It is the only Mediterranean species that is haploxylon excepting *P. cembra,* from which it differs by its shoots.

The wood is not well-known since stands are confined to inaccessible areas. Although available for limited commercial use within close proximity to its stands it is very seldom seen outside the countries in which it grows. The wood is said to be straight-grained but very knotty, and is known to have considerable exudations of strongly odiferous resin.

In the Latin, "peuce" is pronounced "Peu-see"; it is a word used for "pine" or "pitch-pine," which indicates that early authors, as well, were aware of its heavy resinous content. The Greeks still use the resin in their wines *Retsina* and *Roditys* and the flavor it imparts is distinctly like the fragrance of the pine itself.

KEY

Needles:	5 to a sheath, 3-4½″ long, slender, semi-erect on branches, bluish-green; deciduous every 3 yrs.; sharp-pointed apex; stomata on all surfaces and marginal resin canals; basal sheath ¾″ long.
Cones:	Sub-terminal, spreading or pendulous, sub-cylindrical and somewhat curved; 4-6″ long; 1½-2″ wide; brown to yellow, resinous when ripe; scales broadly wedge-shaped; 1¼-1½″ long, ¾″ wide, with a thickened apex; seeds ovoid and small, with short wings, shed when ripe.
Branches:	Smooth green shoots.
Bark:	Dark, reddish-brown to greyish-brown; deeply fissured.
Introduced:	1863

peuce

PINUS MUGO
Mugo Pine; Swiss Mountain Pine

One author swears by *Pinus mugo* (Mugo is the Swiss-Italian vernacular for a particular place—now unknown, but the designation of the pine first appeared in 1764; therefore, it would seem, it should have the advantage of priority); by another, who calls it *P. montanus* (meaning, only, "mountain pine"); by yet another, who considers it to be but a variety of *P. sylvestris,* the Scotch Pine.

Whatever else it is, it is a dwarf. It never grows *up,* only *out.* It survives the salt spray, quite unlike *P. strobus,* and thrives well in what, by any measure, are conditions far different from its native habitat.

It is relatively nondescript: sprawling, bushy, dull-green and dark, small cones, of low and common demeanor, as opposed to stately, tall, and grand.

The books say "generally dwarf—but at times reaching 40 feet." But it is almost always a dwarf. Whatever, it is dense, with stiff compact branches, and looks unsightly when one is broken because you cannot fill the gap.

The wood is negligible as anyone who has cut privet will verify; "wood" except for inferior kindling, is not to be found in shrubs.

There are three major varieties of *P. mugo;* var. *mughus,* var. *uncinata,* and var. *pumilio.* Mirov suggests, also, that at its lower altitudes it may cross naturally with *P. heldreichii* var. *leucodermis.* As well, there are many cultivars of *P. montana.*

KEY

Needles:	2 to a sheath; 1½-3″ long; stiff, curved, dark Hunter green; margins finely-toothed; apex blunt; stomatic lines both surfaces; marginal resin canals; long basal sheath.
Cones:	Solitary or 2-3 together; sub-terminal 1-2″ long, ovoid and symmetrical; short stalks, no prickle; tawny yellow to dark brown; small seeds.
Branches:	Dense, stiff, upright; bushlike.
Bark:	Grey-black, rugose and scaly.
Introduced:	1779

mugo

PINUS MUGO   *Mugo Pine; Swiss Mountain Pine*

PINUS NIGRA *Austrian Pine*

PINUS NIGRA
Austrian Pine

A hardy, rugged pine; very dark and somber inaspect, its dark-green clusters often appearing to be darker than they actually are. In its natural state *P. nigra* is found in the middle altitudes of the northern Italian and Austrian Alps, into the Balkan and Carpathian mountain ranges. Varieties are known also in the Pyrenees and in Corsica.

This tree is dark, forbidding, rough, and coarse but it is widely used for ornamental planting and has become quite popular because of its hardiness and tenacity in the face of modern day pollution. Although it grows to be quite large— 120 to 150 feet in height—it has little value as a timber tree because the wood is coarse and knotty.

Besides being a superior wind-break for situations that require the protection of more fragile trees, the Austrian Pine has the ability, both to succeed on the most meager of soils and, more importantly, to withstand even many of the vitriolic pollutants.

When the conifers died out in Central Park during the early part of this century, until the Arthur Ross Pinetum, *P. nigra* was only one of 3 pine species in the park, and the most numerous by far.

Three principal varieties of the Austrian Pine are still recognized: *P. nigra* var. *caramanica*, Crimean Pine; *P. nigra* var. *cebennensis*, the Pyrenees Pine, usually medium-sized and with a narrow conical crown; and *P. nigra* var. *poiretiana*, the Corsican Pine, tall, erect and more sparsely branched—and therefore the most valuable of all the varieties of *P. nigra*, even more so than the genotype itself. There is a large stand of the variety *poiretiana* in the Bois de Boulogne in Paris.

Because of its wide range throughout the middle-Alpine spine of southern Europe, no single English name is in common use for this species. "Austrian," as we will have it, might just as well read "Italian," "Yugoslavian," or "Carpathian pine," for, as the (nearly always more accurate) scientific appellation would indicate, "black," in whatever local language, is the term most used for this tree. Of course it is not black in actuality, but certainly it is of a darker shade of green than is found in most other pines.

KEY

Needles: 2 to a sheath; very dense, dark green, lacking luster; stiff, straight, stout and curved; 4-6″ long; margins minutely toothed; apex blunt; basal sheath long, wearing away with age.

Cones: Solitary or in clusters; yellow, attached directly to base of branch; ovoid, conical, resinous, 2-3″ long, 1-1½″ wide before opening; scales 1″ long, transversely, near apex with small prickles; seeds greyish-brown, mottled, ⅛″ long, with long wing.

Branches: Yellowish-brown young shoots; ovoid, pointed buds; dense with a tendency to large size; roughened by leaf bases as they grow.

Bark: On old trees, dark brown and deeply fissured into irregular longitudinal, scaly plates—pale brown underneath scales.

Introduced: 1759

austrian/nigra

108

Other Mediterranean Pines

Diploxylon Pines

PINUS BRUTIA
Calabrian Pine

Pinus brutia is often listed as a variety under *P. halepensis*. Its principal variances lie in the needles being longer (4-6″), more rigid, and of a darker green. Also, the cones always are spreading or pointing forwards, never deflexed, as in *P. halepensis*.

PINUS CANARIENSIS
Canary Island Pine

Native to the higher elevations of the Canary Islands, this pine is distinguished from other 3-needled pines by its yellow shoots, fringed bud-scales, long and slender leaves, and large cones. The wood is strong and serviceable, similar to *P. elliottii*, the Slash Pine, but is too rare for export. Basically, it is a sub-tropical pine and generally unsuitable for transplantation in any of the more northerly temperate countries.

Canariensis cone 4-8″

PINUS ELDARICO
(No English Name)

Pinus eldarico—now listed as a separate species—was formerly considered synonymous with *P. brutia* which, as we have seen above, is itself often thought to be synonymous with *P. halepensis*. It would seem—if the current nomenclature is correct—that this pine is purely a rare, desert variety from one locality, only in Tbilisi, Georgia, Transcaucasia, between 600-1,800 feet.

halepensis

heldreichii

var: Leucodermis / Bosnian
cone 3" / needles 1½"
cone is a distinctive
blue-black

heldreichii

pinaster

PINUS HALEPENSIS
Aleppo Pine

Named for a region bordering northern Syria and Turkey, the Aleppo Pine is common in most countries bordering the Mediterranean, from Portugal throughout the Near East. It is recognized by its slender leaves, ash-grey branches, and shining reddish cones. The wood is coarse and resinous and rosin is used as a flavoring in the Greek wines *retsina* and *roditys*. The tree is drought-resistant and hardy, but the wood is of poor quality. Needles 2 to a sheath; slender, curved and twisted; 2-3½" long. Cones pointing downwards, definitely reddish, 2-4½" long, no prickle.

PINUS HELDREICHII
Heldreich Pine

Native to the Balkan Mountains, this is a beautiful, tall and straight tree of up to 70′ in height. Its wood is of fair quality but its isolation discourages much commercial use. The needles are two to a sheath, stiff and sharp-pointed, and bright green. The cones are a glossy yellowish or tawny brown, 3″ long, with a very short, very straight prickle. The bark is grey, flaking off to leave yellowish patches.

PINUS PINASTER
French Maritime Pine

Pinus pinaster is distinguished from other Mediterranean pines by its very thick, deeply-fissured, reddish bark; by its long, stout needles; and by its persistant cones. In the Landes district of France, this heavily-resinous, densely-planted tree is tapped after the fashion of rubber trees, with diagonal slashes draining into buckets, and later allowed to heal and to be recut yet again. This tree is the primary turpentine tree of Europe, where the Landes, like the American South, has for years used it as a principal bulwark of its economy.

Pinus pinaster is a tall tree 90-120′ high, and often quite bare of branches for most of its length. Needles are 2 to a sheath; stout, rigid and curved; 7-10″ long. Cones are bright brown and shining, 5-10″ long, and are often in large clusters.

PINUS PINEA
Italian Stone Pine

Pinus pinea was named by Linnaeus as the "Pine of Pines" because it has been extensively planted for centuries all along the Mediterranean coast from Portugal to the Near East. It is known for its peculiar umbrella-shaped crown, large and round, symmetrical cones, and for its edible nuts. It is a familiar ornamental tree in many Mediterranean localities but particularly loved and cultivated in Italy. The tree itself is picturesque and most distinct in its habitat, to 80′ in height and nearly always with flat, very dense, spreading crown. The needles are 2 to a sheath, slightly twisted, and 4½-6″ long. The globose cones ripen every third year, are shining nut-brown, erect on stout stalks and are 4-6″ long and at least 4″ wide. The edible seeds are large and numerous—often numbering over 100 in a cone; they are dark, ⅝-¾″ long, purplish-brown, with a thick shell and an edible kernel. *Pinocchi* is one of the numerous names for pine kernels in Italy. *Pinocchio*—whom we all know—was either called by that name possibly because he was carved from the wood *P. pinea,* or, more likely, Gepetto named him because he was a "pine nut". At any rate, both he and the tree are favorites over the years.

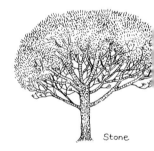

Stone

PINUS PITYUSA
Pityunda Pine

This pine is named—with uncharacteristic consideration for more humanistic appeal than is found in most latter-day scientific nomenclature—for Pitys, the tragic nymph of Greek mythology. Again, like *P. brutia,* this pine is almost synonymous with *P. halepensis,* the Aleppo Pine, except for its shorter (1½-2″ long) needles. It is found only in the Aegean region.

PINUS SYLVESTRIS *Scotch Pine*

Northern Eurasian Pines

PINUS SYLVESTRIS
Scotch Pine

This is the pine of northern Europe. *P. sylvestris* is found, in greater or lesser abundance, from northern Sweden to the mountains of Spain, and from the shores of the North Sea across the millions of square miles of Russian taiga to Kamchatka and the shores of the Pacific. As well, it is hardy, vigorous and has been planted throughout the world in most temperate climates.

P. sylvestris (meaning forest-loving) is the true fir (*fur, fura*) of the old Norsemen and Viking ships, Baltic ships of commerce, and millions of wooden homes and structures from Stavangerfjord across to Mora in Sweden, past Turku, Leningrad, Moscow, and all the way to Vladivostock, where they were, and are, fashioned mostly from this tree. The name "Scotch Fir" persisted well into this century for many years after it was botanically known to be a pine and not a fir. The tree is of such value to so many countries that each country would seem to claim it as its own with their chosen ethnic name: "Bois rouge du Nord," "Pin de Genvre," "Weiss-Keifer," "Riga Fir," "Norway Fir," "Polish Fir," etc.—all quite the same tree.

When I first crossed central Sweden by train, along with countless moose (Älg) tracks in the snow, fox tracks, and cross-country skiers' tracks, there were miles upon miles of monotonous tall pines that no doubt had some "disease"— some blight or other, I imagined. So distressed was I that so much of Sweden was "losing its forests" that I mentioned it to more than one person. They all looked at me as though I had two heads. 'Wrong? There is something wrong?'

What was "wrong" was that everything was quite all right. The Scotch Pine is the only pine that has, on the lower part of its trunk, a decidedly "piney-look" of proper grey-brown bark, reasonably fissured into irregular plates. But about one-half to two-thirds up the tree, the bark changes to a light red or orange, shining and kept as fresh as paint by the continual process of shedding its papery scales. The effect can be startling to one unaquainted with it.

This tree is most commonly only 70 to 100 feet in height, but can grow to 150 feet high. It has a straight trunk; stiff, twisted, grey-green needles and in spring the male catkins, in dense whorls, fill the air with their sulphurlike pollen.

In its feral state *P. sylvestris* shelters untold millions of small feathered and furred creatures and feeds even more with its dark, nutritious seeds; not least among which is the European Red Squirrel, *Sciurus vulgaris*, with its long ear tufts and pert, intelligent expression.

immature Scots

KEY

Needles: 2 to a sheath; 1-4″ long, but variable in length; short, stiff, twisted, grey-green; short-pointed; resin canals marginal and minutely toothed; basal sheath at first white and ⅓″ long; to later become grey and shorter.

Cones: Mainly solitary or 2-3 together; 1-3″ long, greyish or dark brown, but variable in shape although usually oval, short stalks; scales narrow and oblong, with a minute prickle; seed ellipsoid, $^1/_8$-$^1/_5$″ long, dark with long wing.

Branches: Whorled in younger trees, but in age branching only at the upper trunk and growing into a mushroomlike top.

scots
(mature)

Bark: Grey-brown and fissured on first ½-⅔ of tree length, then becoming light red to orange, shining, and sealing off in the thin, papery scales. The effect of the glaucous green leaves contrasting strongly with the fiery red-orange upper bark is a helpful identification aid.

Introduction: unknown

Other Northern Eurasian Pines

Haploxylon Pines

PINUS PUMILA
Japanese Stone Pine

Pinus pumila, a natural dwarf, is hardly ever more than 10 feet high. In its native Siberia or on the frigid islands of northern Japan, it grows in the coldest and most unexplored of locations, sometimes forming dense, impenetrable thickets. The tree has no commerical value and is hardly ever seen in ornamental use outside *pineta*. The needles are 5 to a sheath, resembling *P. cembra,* but shorter and more slender. The 2″-long orangebrown cones never open but depend upon foraging birds and animals to disperse them.

pumila

PINUS SIBIRICO
Siberian Pine

This tall tree—to 130′ in height—also resembles *P. cembra,* and is sometimes regarded as a variety. It is so like *P. cembra* that it needs nothing more than a referral to that species— except for its distribution. It is a native only of N.E. Russia. The edible seeds are widely used in the U.S.S.R.

115

Southeastern Asian Pines

PINUS ARMANDI
Chinese White Pine

Native to the mountains of Western China, the Chinese White Pine is widely distributed but seldom forms large forests. It favors rocky, subalpine habitats and was discovered by Père Armand David—the Père David of Père David's Deer—in Shensi Province in 1873, but was later found to cover wide areas of China and Korea.

Because of its fast growth and classically triangular shape, this pine is frequently planted as an ornamental tree. It grows to 60 feet and has wide-spreading horizontal branches and bright green foliage.

Pinus armandi resembles *P. wallichiana,* the Himalayan Pine, in general form and coloration, but the distinct ben in the needle in *P. armandi* is lacking in *P. wallichiana.* Also, the cones are quite distinctively different, those of the Chinese Pine being stouter and the scales much wider than those of the Himalayan Pine.

KEY

Needles: 5 to a sheath; slender and thin, drooping ("weeping") and wide-spreading; 4-6" long, sharply bent ½-¾" from base; bright green under surface, 2 upper surfaces white with stomatic lines and 3 resin canals; deciduous every 2-3 years.

Cones: Sub-terminal on 1" stalks; 1-3 together, broadly cylindrical tapering to a rounded apex, 4-7" long and 2-3½" wide; at first erect, then pendulous in second year; yellowish-brown; seeds pale reddish-brown, ovoid and compressed, ½" long with sharp edgem

Branches: Greenish, with smooth surface, usually minutely glandular.

Bark: Thin, smooth, greenish.

Introduced: 1895

armandii

PINUS ARMANDI   *Chinese White Pine*

PINUS BUNGEANA *Lace-bark Pine*

PINUS BUNGEANA
Lace-bark Pine

The Lace-bark Pine, named for Dr. Alexander von Bunge who first discovered it in 1831, is a singularly interesting tree even in its native China where, for centuries, it has been cultivated in the vicinity of burial grounds and temples. Its name is derived from the scaling-off of the dull grey bark in small patches, after the fashion of a sycamore or eucalyptus, revealing an inner bark that, in young trees, is decidedly lacelike in appearance and, in older trees, can become nearly all chalk-white and readily recognizable at some distance.

This tree appears to have been always of somewhat limited abundance in its native habitat but has been carefully cultivated not only in China but in most temperate regions of the world wherever nurserymen and botanists are to be found. It is more or less conical but more bushlike in cultivation, often with multiple trunks; and, in China, reaches heights of 80 to 100 feet. In this country, however, it is generally much less tall. It is related to the Himalayan Chilghoza Pine, *Pinus gerardiana*, but has smaller cones and stiffer needles. It is slow-growing with rather sparse, light-green foliage.

Note: It seems a curious thing that in its native habitat *P. bungeana* should be growing, as does our own rare fern the Purple Cliffbrake, *Pellaea atropurpurea*, in areas of limestone rocks, which, in many a circumstance, also show a startling degree of whiteness from a distance. And not infrequently will its branches shelter the Waxwing, *Bombycilla garrulus*.

KEY

Needles: 3 to a sheath; sparsely arranged on branches; deciduous every 5 years; light-green, rather stiff, flattened, 2-3" long; margins finely-toothed, apex sharply-pointed, prominent marginal resin canals; gives off odor of turpentine when bruised.

Cones: Solitary or in pairs; on very short, stout stalks; either globular or ovoid, 2-2½" long; light yellowish-brown, no prickle; seed dark brown with short, narrow, loosely-attached wing, ⅓-½" long.

Branches: Long and slender, greyish-green.

Bark: Exfoliation of dull grey bark in irregular plates exposes inner bark which varies from silver-blue, to greenish-blue, to light brown, to whitish, to (in age) a chalky-white.

Introduced: 1846

Lacebark Grove

PINUS DENSIFLORA
Japanese Red Pine

Pinus densiflora is very much like *P. sylvestris,* the Scotch Pine, but having more slender, dull green needles, greenish branchlets, and larger cones. The Japanese Red Pine is a tree that grows from 70-120 feet in height, but unlike the Scotch Pine it is frequently twisted and crooked instead of arrow-straight. It is interesting to note that this pine—again, like *P. sylvestris*—has the reddish bark, above a certain height, peeling off in thin scales.

The wood, too, is comparable to the Scotch Pine, being of good quality, moderately-hard, strong and resinous. It does not, however, hold well in the ground; if used there it must be thoroughly creosoted. The roots are highly resinous and are often split into sections to use as torches—for instance, by the cormorant fisherman. Also, under the forest canopy of stands of *P. densiflora,* one of the most popular of the edible fungi, "Matsutake," is carefully cultivated and harvested.

The Japanese Red Pine is the most common tree of Japan and, in that country occupies a similar position to that of *P. sylvestris* in Northern Europe. *P. densiflora* has seven varieties which vary greatly in color and shape.

KEY

densiflora

Needles:	2 to a sheath; deciduous every 3 years; slender, soft, twisted, dull green; 2-4½" long; finely-toothed margins; stomata on both surfaces; marginal resin canals.
Cones:	Sub-terminal; solitary or in clusters of 2-3; grey or brownish; larger than Scotch Pine; seed, ¼" long with well-developed wing.
Branches:	Young shoots without down, green with greenish-blue hue.
Bark:	Reddish; scales peeling on the upper portions of tree, often the fashion of Scotch Pine.
Introduced:	?

120

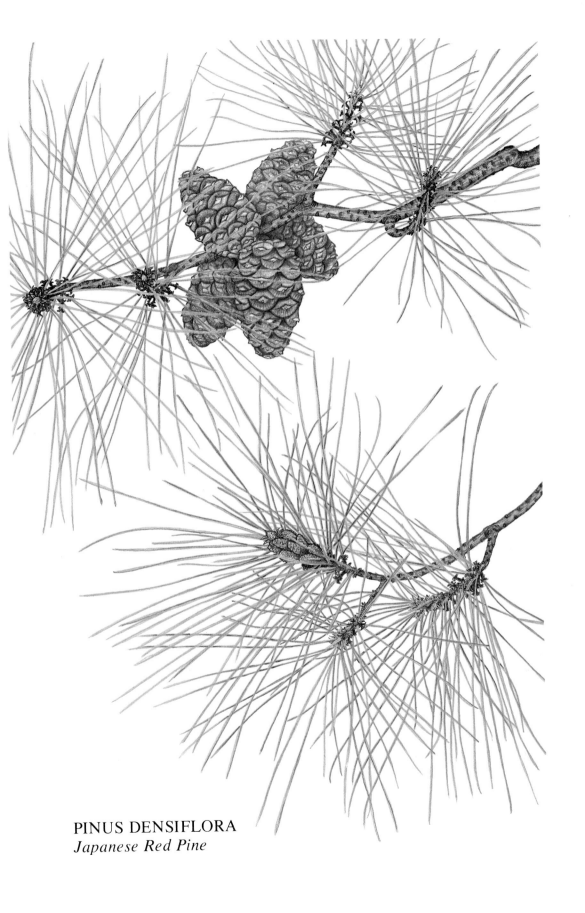

PINUS DENSIFLORA
Japanese Red Pine

PINUS WALLICHIANA *Himalayan Pine*

PINUS WALLICHIANA
Himalayan Pine

From 50-150 feet in height, this pine of the temperate Himalayan regions from Nepal and Bhutan to Afghanistan, named after Nathaniel Wallich (1786–1854), a Danish botanist, is an elegant and beautiful tree because of its large, horizontal lower branches, wide-spreading needle-fronds and smooth cones. It is used worldwide in temperate zones as a decorative tree and—surprisingly, considering the clarity and antiseptic quality of its native health—it withstands atmospheric pollution better than most pines.

There are two varieties of *Pinus Wallichiana*, var. *monophylla*, which has single needles welded together, and var. *zebrina*, in which the needles are barred with alternate green and gold.

In New York City, the finest example of the Himalayan Pine is to be found in Prospect Park. It is over 100 years old—going back to the beginning of the park in 1866.

Note: Next to one of the True Cedars, *Pinus Wallichana* (also called *Pinus griffithii*) is the most important timber tree of the Himalayas, the wood being durable and working well in carpentry. Also, its resin is tapped after the fashion of rubber trees, running freely from diagonal cuts incised in the bark. These tapping operations last three years and then the tree is given three years rest before tapping begins again. Its rosin and turpentine are of the most excellent quality.

KEY

Needles: 5 to a sheath; deciduous 3-4 years; slender, bluish-green on one side and silvery on the other; slightly bent and drooping, ⅝" long; finely-toothed margins and sharply-pointed apex; white stomatic lines on flat surface; marginal resin canals; white basal sheath ¾" long.

Cones: Sub-terminal; solitary or in pairs; ovoid, pendulous after second year; light brown; 6-12" long, 1½" wide; very resinous; no prickles; on stalks 1½-2" long; scales broad and wedge-shaped with exposed portion grooved; seeds ovoid with ¾-1" wing; empty cones remain on tree for several month before falling.

Branches: Young shoots without down, greenish, darkening with age; branches thin and smooth, and lower branches spreading horizontally while upper branches ascending.

Bark: Smooth and resinous in youth; greyish-brown and only shallowly fissured on old trees.

Introduced: 1827

Wallichiana
HIMALAYAN

123

PINUS PARVIFLORA
Japanese White Pine

At best a medium-sized tree, 20 to 50 feet tall, the Japanese White Pine is short-needled and small-coned and is cultivated mostly for its picturesque habit of pyramidal growth. It is indeed a hardy and handsome pine with excessively wide-spreading branches and dark green foliage. It is much sought after and cultivated in dwarf form for use as Bonsai. It has two varieties: var. *breviflora* and var. *glauca*. each of which is not demonstrably different than the species beyond a shade of color and a stiffer quality to the needles.

The wood is straight-grained but not available in long lengths because of its tendency to form a short trunk with wide-spreading branches. The wood is used for general carpentry close to its native stands in Japan but is not exported.

This tree is most common in the Japanese mountain forests above 5,000 feet. It is still referred to by the name *P. parviflora* (because of its small flowers), but *P. himekomatsu* is currently an accepted nomenclatory designation.

KEY

parviflora

Needles: 5 to a sheath; deciduous every 3-4 years; 2-3" long, slender and curved with blunt apex; inner flat surface with 3-4 prominent stomatic lines, giving appearance of green on one side, "silvery" on the other; marginal resin canals.

Cones: Solitary or in clusters; ovoid and erect, 2-2½" long, 1-1¼" wide; few scales, leathery, and broadly wedge-shaped; seed small with narrow wing.

Branches: Young trees conical, older trees with widely spreading branches.

Bark: Thin, smooth and greyish; becoming scaly on older trees.

Introduced: 1861

PINUS PARVIFLORA *Japanese White Pine*

PINUS KORAIENSIS *Korean Pine*

PINUS KORAIENSIS
Korean Pine

Not only found in Korea, this pine is widely distributed in eastern Asia. In Japan the tree is often found more frequently intermixed with deciduous trees than in isolated forests. Similar to *P. cembra*, the Swiss Stone Pine, this tree differs from it by its longer needles and white inner surface; the resin canals number 3 to *P. cembra's* 2; and the cones are longer with less obvious outlines. This tree can be quite tall—from 100-150 feet in height.

The wood is soft and light, straight-grained and easily worked in carpentry. It more resembles *P. strobus* in quality than does any other oriental pine. It is exported in great quantity from its native countries and is an important commercial tree.

In Korea and China it grows in the mountain areas that are home to the Blue-eared Pheasant, one of the world's most strikingly beautiful birds.

KEY

Needles: 5 to a sheath; 2½-5″ long; dark green on one side, silvery the other; longer and more spreading than *P. cembra;* sharply-toothed margins, blunt apex; 3 resin canals; numerous stomatic lines cause silvery appearance on under side.

Cones: Sub-terminal; erect; conic-oblong or cylindrical, blunt at the apex; yellowish-brown; 5-6″ long; short stalks; leathery with waxy margin; seeds ½″ long, wingless.

Branches: Spreading or erect and yellow-brown.

Bark: Thin, reddish-grey, smooth; somewhat scaly in age.

Introduced: 1861

Koraiensis

PINUS TABULAEFORMIS *Chinese Pine*

PINUS TABULAEFORMIS
Chinese Pine

This is a diploxylon, i.e. "hard" pine, and is a medium-sized tree of the foothills of China and Korea. It is often confused with the Japanese Black Pine, *P. thunbergii,* but is easily distinguished from that pine by the color of the buds and principally, by the color of the cones, pale tawny, changing to nut-brown as opposed, in *R. thunbergii,* to a definite reddish-brown. Also, *tabulaeformis* refers to its crown being like a table.

This tree is not an important timber tree and is not exported. It is the common pine of the mountains of the Szechwan Province—where the food is spicy, perhaps to ward off the mountain chill. This pine has only one variety, differing in the length of the cones. *P. tabulaeformis* var. *densata* differs in its oblique cones which are swollen in thin terminal ends, and is a high altitude tree from western Szechwan. Another, former variety, has been given specific rank: *P. yunnanensis.*

KEY

Needles:	2 (sometimes 3) to a sheath (often varying on the same tree); dark green, densely-crowded on the branches; 4-6″ long; margins finely toothed; stomatic lines on both surfaces.
Cones:	Ovoid, up to 2″ long; "scales with terminal portion shining, pale tawny yellow at first, gradually changing to a dark nut brown."
Branches:	Flat-crowned and gnarled.
Bark:	Usually grey—but occasionally red and peeling in thin sheets.
Introduced:	1862

tabuliformis/CHINESE

129

PINUS THUNBERGII
Japanese Black Pine

This is a fair-sized tree, up to 130 feet high with a girth of 20 feet. The branches are stout and twisted, forming an irregular crown. It is a tree that has been, in its native Japan, so carefully cultivated for many years that its origins are difficult to define. It is so picturesque and so hardy that it is constantly being raised for ornamental purposes in many parts of the world's temperate zones. *Pinus thunbergii* is distinguished from *P. tabulaeformis* by its conspicuous white buds and rigid needles.

The Japanese Black Pine is one of the most important of Japan's timber trees and is also widely used for reclaiming sand dunes at the ocean's edge because of its hardiness in the face of salt-water spray. This pine is also used extensively for Bonsai culture.

P. thunbergii flourishes on Martha's Vineyard in Nantucket and is planted on New York City beaches and at Riis Park. This tree was named after Dr. Carl Peter Thunberg (1743-1828), of Sweden, a student of Linnaeus who traveled extensively in Java and in Japan.

KEY

Needles:	2 to a sheath; deciduous every 3 years; 3-5" long, densely-crowded, spreading rigid, and twisted; dark green—"black" after the fashion of the Austrian Pine; margins finely-toothed; stiffly-pointed apex; stomatic lines on each surface; basal sheath long, ending in two white filaments.
Cones:	Sub-terminal; solitary or 2-3 together or in large clusters of 40-60 or more; reddish to nut brown; transversely-keeled and flat or curved; 2½" long; short stalks; small prickles; seed small, with narrow wing.
Branches:	Young shoots light brown to orange-yellow; ridged; older branches rugose from leaf scars.
Bark:	Greyish-brown, deeply fissured.
Introduced:	?

thunbergi

130

PINUS THUNBERGII   *Japanese Black Pine*

Other Southeastern Asian Pines
Haploxylon Pines

PINUS DALATENSIS
(No English Name)

A little-known pine from southern Vietnam. It appears to be *Pinus strobus*-like; a White Pine. It was collected from only two localities at altitudes of 4,500 to 7,500 feet.

PINUS FENZELIANA
(No English Name)

A doubtful species and is being only tentatively considered as a valid entity. This pine is from the Luichou-Peninsula of Kwangtung Province in China.

gerardiana

PINUS GERARDIANA
Ghilghoza Pine

This is a 3 to a sheath haploxylon pine which is native to eastern Afghanistan and Baluchistan (the latter now partly Pakistanian) and adjacent parts of India. It is essentially a high-altitude pine and is not well-known.

PINUS KWANGTUNGENSIS
(No English Name)

This pine from Kwangtung and southern Hunan Provinces in China is another tree that is not well-known and is also open to controversy as a species. It is generally found at an altitude of 3,000 feet and is said to resemble *P. parviflora*.

PINUS MORRISONICOLA
(No English Name)

Pinus morrisonicola is from Formosa (Taiwan) and is closely related to *P. parviflora*, the Japanese White Pine. It is found at altitudes from 900-7,000 feet. The chemistry of this pine is said to suggest that it hybridizes with *P. armandi*, the Chinese White Pine.

PINUS PENTAPHYLLA
Japanese White Pine (synonymous with *P.parviflora* in the vernacular)

Another controversial pine: it is said that on the island of Honshu it crosses with *P. parviflora*. Most of these "difficult" pines come into the realm of chemical analysis because they are all physically similar.

Diploxylon Pines

PINUS FUNEBRIS
(No English Name)

This diploxylon pine is closely allied to *P. densiflora*. It is from northern Korea and is a pine of low elevations even to sea level near the Russo-Korean border.

PINUS HWANGSHANENSIS
(No English Name)

Another (until recently) politically-affected pine from east central China, this is a tree apparently confined to the higher elevations and is of uneven distribution.

PINUS INSULARIS
Luzon Pine

A pine of the Phillipines, *P. insularis* forms extensive forest in the highlands of northern Luzon. Again, its positive identity by way of specific isolation is often in doubt, sometimes considered to be *P. khasya*.

PINUS KHASYA
Khasia Pine

From Thailand, India, Burma, Laos, and southern Vietnam this pine is often called *P. insularis*. It is a strong and definitely isolated species—but it is up to the taxonomist to decide precisely what it is and to which others it may be related. Clearly, all we can say here is that it exists.

Luchensis/ BURMA

PINUS LUCHUENSIS
Okinawa Pine

Extending from Okinawa down the chain of the Ryukyu Islands this tree prefers only moderately-high elevations and can, and does, thrive in areas of low elevation. Usually it is of contorted form because of the force of maritime winds. Needles are in pairs, 6-8″ long. Cones are symmetrical, 2″ long, and shining nut-brown.

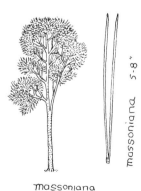

massoniana

PINUS MASSONIANA
Masson Pine

Chinese authors call this the "southern red pine." It covers large areas of Szechwan and many other provinces of interior China. It is quite an attractive pine, being rounded on the top and branching out from about one half its total height. Needles occur in pairs, are 6-8″ long, and yellowish-green. Cones are small, falling early, and dark brown in color.

PINUS MERKUSII
Merkus Pine

This pine is from the southern Shan state of Burma and it crosses over into northern Thailand, and into Vietnam. It is the only pine that naturally crosses the Equator—in a tiny square of Sumatra known as the Barisan Range. Needles are 2 to a sheath and 7-10″ long; cones are 2-3″ long, narrowly-cylindrical and often curved. This species is clearly known by its leaf sections and by its peculiar cones. This is the most tropical of all pines.

PINUS ROXBURGHII
Chir Pine

From the foothills of the Himalayas, this tall pine is quite handsome, being straight and arrowlike with a light and airy crown of tender green. This tree occurs also on Formosa. Needles are 3 to a bundle, light green, long and slender, 9-13″ long. Cones are large, 4-8″ long, and ovoid on short stalks.

Roxburghii - Chir

PINUS TAIWANENSIS
Formosa Pine

This straight and tall tree of the island of Formosa (Taiwan) is a pine of high elevation and stands of it cover large areas of the mountainous parts of the island.

Taiwanensis

PINUS YUNNANENSIS
YUNNAN Pine

The Yunnan-Kewichow Plateau of southwestern China is the native home of this pine. There are very few growths of it below 1,500 feet and it ascends, in places, to over 12,000 feet. Needles are 3 to a bundle, up to 10″ long, and long and drooping. Some authors consider this e a variety of *P. tabulaeformis,* the Chinese Pine.

135

Quite separated from the necessities of modern-day living in which the Pine has a part, i.e., lumber (which is sawn timber); naval stores; newspapers, paper towels, soft tissues and countless books from southern pulp; down to wine-flavoring and edible nuts, this family of useful trees has an even more powerful elixir for the soul of contemporary man. That potent vehicle is *romanticism*. Modern Man may buy and sell wooden houses, consume millions of tons of paper, and expand most forcefully on the attributes of timber shares; but, alone in a mood of reflection, he will tell you of the elemental charm of wood smoke, of the essential fragrance of pine wood, and of the overwhelming beauty of pine branches as they curve in graceful arcs against the first soft stars of a summer night. The beauty of form, and scent, and of gentle movement inherent in these trees has captured not only poets, arborists and gardeners, but anyone whose heart and mind is not hewn from senseless stone or molded from lifeless steel.

"A garden is the mirror of a mind." (Anon.) is a thought-provoking quotation and pines have been among the most useful of garden backdrops and complimentary ornamentations since early time. The *pineta* (pinetums) of European parks, public estates, and private houses are manifold. The Orient is filled with little parks and vistas featuring only pines and bare stone—and for what reasons?—for human enrichment. Fountains, vistas, flower borders—all are enhanced by the use of pines as a background.

But what of our own "estates"—not (these days) perhaps necessarily large and spacious? If we love pines, can we not have our own *pineta?* That has been, I think, the primary purpose of this book—to know each pine for what it is; and its usefulness is dictated *by what it is*. A pinetum—and a good and proper one—can consist of only three trees, but trees *well-chosen*. An half-acre of land (sensibly used) can be home to a surprising number of beautiful pines—and that, again, is why we have considered the species in some depth. Their height, their breadth, their hues, their configuration and all pertinent considerations of their growth and use can, and should, influence our choices in transplantation. The most lacklustre of structures, locations and neighborhood environments, which often in these times of overcrowding, have forced us to limit our ambitions in the way of what is somewhat commercially abused in the appellation of "gracious living," can be blunted (if not wholly overcome) by the use of pines to "plant-out" whatever it is we might not wish to see.

Even a single pine, transplanted and cared-for, can lift one's spirits—and given, in addition, a few choice perennials in a tiny border, and allowing room for annuals in a box or two, a garden is brought to fruition.

Size is not important in the timeless presence of a hand-woven oriental carpet, nor in the delicate tracery of silver filagree—neither is size a factor in the confines of a pinetum. If one loves pines, one can *have* pines—only in proportion to one's ability to keep them.

Size *is* the crux in regard to the number of pines in a *pinetum*. One must remember that pines (and other trees, for that matter if you have a turn in that direction) grow—not only *up*, but most decidely *out*. One plants a pine, not by its size when transplantable but by what its genetic makeup dictates it will become. And, today, we have learned enough to predict what that will be. And so, in planning, one must carefully consider the results of overcrowding and ruinous lack of foresight. For example, an half-acre consists of 21,780 square feet. Within that square (presuming it to be square) only so many reasonably-sized circles (the diameter of an adult tree) will fit. A potted, out-of-the-nursery pine may measure twelve inches in diameter at its arrival home. But, given fifteen years of growth, it can measure thirty feet across. Suddenly, in comprehension of this, that "large" half-acre most considerably shrinks in size.

The answer to profitable space usage is planning. You now have the answers to *which* pines will best suit your needs. Transplantation and an initial watering program—with perhaps a modicum of judicious feeding—will make of your acreage, large or small, precisely what you will have it: as a screen, or a background, or, in the end, simply a presence-in-itself of fragrant pines.

We have spoken of romanticism and do again, for there are far more B.T.U.s in the tender presence of a loved one than can be calculated by any thermal measuring device. If one is immune to the spell of Robert Frosts's:

> "When there was no more light in the kitchen,
> The fire got out through crannies in the stove
> And danced in yellow wrigglers on the ceiling,
> As much at home as if they'd always danced there."

—then perhaps further mention of firelight, crackling flames, hot cider and the warmth of companionship is a redundancy not to be borne.

On the other hand, we have touched upon a rather cold-blooded cadence of calculation: the effect of terpenes and heptanes; the elasticity of wood at 1,540,000 lbs per square inch; about comparative strength of compression and tension; and of chromosomal microscopy of the pine. Is there less poetry in these aspects of inquiry than in the above quotation? Robert Frost—I cannot help but think—would not have thought so.

The giant companies that deal in the assets of timber do, indeed, upon occasion, demand and get through political activity, certain tracts for commercial purposes—tracts that might well have been preserved. It is often overlooked, however, that these same companies have reseeded and nurtured literally millions of square miles of devastated land that will, one day, again be fragrant pine forests. Whether or not these forests are only to be reused for profit is hardly our concern. They are renewed; they are renewable. As the cycle of industry goes on, more and more of these companies are employing the services of horticultural scientists, whose advice (even though profitable gain may be the only motive) is being listened to and appropriate conservatory action is being applied. Crude oil, for instance, is a finite resource; pines are a renewable resource.

The purpose of the Arthur Ross Pinetum in Central Park (New York City)—only one amongst others in this country and around the world—is an ional institution in itself. It teaches only one course and does not give out diplomas; but the lessons of conservation, ecological balance, and the vision of renewal it embraces make of it a most valued and worthwhile experiment—something of value for humanity at all ages.

As for further enquiry into this subject, I will suggest that no better beginning might be made than to read Dr. Nicholas T. Mirov's and Jean Hasbrouck's small volume, *The Story of Pines,* published in 1976 by the Indiana University Press. Also, Dr. Mirov's, *The Genus Pinus,* Ronald Press, New York, 1967, is certainly among the most lucid, as well as the most thorough, of any of the definitive volumes—even though, as Dr. Mirov himself states, "There are no books in which all aspects of the whole genus *Pinus* are included."

Addenda

Coulteri

Name adopted from that of John Merle Coulter, 1851–1928, American botanist and author of botanical manuals

Torreyana

Name taken from that of John Torrey, 1796–1873, a New York botanist and chemist, a prolific writer whose admirers, in his life time, founded the Torrey Botanical Club which was largely instrumental in establishing the New York Botanical Garden

taeda: another latin name for pine

balfouri

Sir Isaac Bayley Balfour, 1853–1922, Professor of Botany and Keeper of the Royal Botanical Garden at Edinburg, founder of *Annals of Botany.*

cembroides: a Pinus cembroides is a species which resembles the Pinus cembra. . . .

Glossary of Terms

aldehyde chemical compound derived from alcohol combined with an acid

alkaloid nitrogenous base usually of vegetable origin, having a physiological effect on animals and humans

alpine inhabiting or growing in mountainous regions above the limits of forest growths

amino acids any of a group of organic compounds forming an essential part of protein molecules

apex the highest point; tip; top

arboretum a botanical garden exhibiting trees for their scientific interest

asymmetrical unbalanced spatial arrangements

bark covering of the stems, branches and roots of a tree or other plant, as distinguished from wood

biennial occurring every second year; a plant that produces flowers and fruits in its second year

biochemistry branch of chemistry relating to the processes and physical properties of living organisms

bonsai a potted plant (as a tree) dwarfed by special methods of culture

borneol transluscent crystalline solid found in cavities in the trunk of a large tree

botanist one versed in botany, the study of plants

bract a modified leaf in a flower cluster or subtending a flower

B.T.U. British thermal unit— that amount of heat required to raise the temperature of one pound of water one degree Fahrenheit

cambium a layer of tissue in plants from which new bark and wood are formed

carene either of two liquid terpenes found in some turpentine oils

catharsis purging, especially the alimentary canal

chlorophyll the green coloring matter contained in the chloroplasts of plants; essential to the production of carbohydrates by photosynthesis

chromosomes rod-shaped bodies into which the chromatin of the cell nucleus divide during cell division; contain the genes, the determiners of heredity

classification the sorting into classes on the basis of similarities and differences

cluster a collection of objects of the same kind; to grow or form into a cluster

cold stratification the process of storing seeds at reduced temperatures in preparation for planting

concentric having a common center, as a circle

cones a dry multiple fruit, as of a pine, composed of scales arranged symmetrically around an axis and enclosing seeds

conifer any of a large and widely distributed family of evergreen shrubs and trees characterized by needle-shaped leaves, cones and a resinous wood

coniferous cone-bearing

cotyledons first leaves from a sprouting seed

crenulated finely notched or scalloped, as some leaves

crop the cultivated produce of the land as grain, vegetables or trees

crossbreeding interbreeding of two varieties

cultivar a horticulture variety of a plant or flower

cyclitols polyhydroxyl compounds

deciduous a falling off at maturity or specific seasons, as petals, fruits, or leaves

decurrent extending or running downward into another structure, as the base of a leaf into the stem

dendrochronologist one who studies the annual rings of trees

dendrologist one who studies trees

dendrology the branch of botany and forestry that deals with trees

diploxylon name given to those pines of which a cross section of the needle shows two vascular bundles

dormant not active; marked by partial suspension of vital processes, as are many plants and animals in winter

ellipsoid a solid of which every plane section is an ellipse or circle

embryo the earliest stages in the development of an organism, before it has assumed its distinctive form

endosperm the nutritive substance within the embryo sac of an ovule

ester any of a class of organic compounds formed by the reaction of an acid with an alcohol, with the elimination of water

evergreen having foliage that remains green until the formation of new foliage

exfoliation to separate or peel off in scale, layers, flakes, etc., as skin, bark or bone

exudation act of exuding, such as resin or sweat

feral wild; not tamed or domesticated

fissure a narrow opening, cleft, crevice or furrow

foliage the growth of leaves on a tree or other pant

forest canopy a formation of branches affording a cover of foliage

genera plural of genus

genetics the science dealing with the interaction of

genes producing similarities and differences between individuals

genotype the genetic constitution of an organism

genus a grouping of plants and animals next above species and next below family or subfamily

germination to begin to grow; sprout

glaucous green having a yellowish-green color; covered with a whitish bloom

globose spherical

globular formed of globules

haploxylon name given to those pines of which a cross section of the needle shows only one vascular bundle

heartwood the darker central portion of a tree trunk

heptane a colorless flammable liquid hydrocarbon used as a solvent

horticulture the art or science of cultivating plants

hybrid an organism produced by breeding a male and female of different species, varieties or breeds

internecine destructive to both sides; mutually deadly

kernel the entire contents of a seed of grain within its coating

ketone one of a class of organic compounds in which the carbonyl radical unites with two hydrocarbon radicals

lignin an organic substance that together with cellulose makes up the essential part of woody tissue

limonene aromatic terpene, occurring in various es-

sential oils, as of oranges, lemons, etc.

maritime headlands a cliff projecting into the water

mesa a high, broad and flat tableland with sharp, usually rocky, slopes descending to the surrounding plains

miniscule of very small size and importance

morphology study of the form and structure of plants and animals considered apart from function

nomenclature the system of names used to describe the various elements of science; terminology

nursery a place where trees, shrubs, etc. are grown for sale or transplantation

ovoid egg-shaped

paleobotanical relating to the study of fossil plants

pelage the coat or covering of a mammal, as fur, wool, etc.

pendulous hanging

perennials continuing through many years; a plant that grows for three or more years but usually blooming or fruiting each year

phloem complex plant tissue composed of sieve tubes with associated cells for conducting sap

photosynthesis process by which green plants form carbohydrates from carbon dioxide and water through the agency of sunlight acting upon chlorophyll

pinetum a plantation of pine trees

pollution refuse of noxious materials that impair the purity of water, soil, or atmosphere

prickle small, sharp point, as on the bark or cone of a plant

propagates to cause (animals, plants, etc.) to multiply by natural reproduction; to reproduce itself

pubescent to grow hair

pulp a moist, soft mixture of wood fibers or rags to form substance of paper

rejuvenation to give new vigor; to restore

resin an amorphous organic substance exuded from plants, especially from firs or pine trees

respiration process by which a plant or aimal takes in oxygen from the air and gives off carbon dioxide and other products of oxidation

rosin the hard amber-colored residue after the distillation of turpentine from resin

rugose covered with or full of wrinkles; having a rough surface

sap aqueous juices of plants that contain the materials necessary for plant growth

sapling a young tree

sapwood the new wood just inside the bark

scales rudimentary or metamorphosed woody bract of a pine cone

scion a detached living portion of a plant to be grafted onto a stock of another

seedling a plant grown from a seed as distinguished from propagated by grafting; a very small or young plant

senescent growing old; characteristic of old age

somnolent inclined to sleep; drowsy

species a category of plants and animals subordinate to the genus but above a breed, race, strain or variety

staminate having stamens but no pistils

stands the growing trees in a forest or part of a forest

stomata plural of stoma; small pores or openings in the epidermis of plants, especially of leaves and stems

stratify to form or arrange in layers

subalpine region in mountains near but below the timber line

subtropical region intermediate between the torrid and temperature zones

symbiotic mutually advantageous partnership

symmetrical having parts or organs on one side corresponding to those on the other in size, shape, function, structure, etc.; regular as to numbers or shapes of parts

tableland flat topped elevation

tapping an arrangement for drawing out liquid; to *tap* a sugar maple or pine

taxonomist a student of taxonomy

taxonomy the systematic arrangement of plants and animals according to established criteria that determines their assignment to the following major groups: kingdom, phylum, class, order, family, genus and species

tenacious stubborn, obstinate; to hold strongly

terminal shoot borne at end of stem or branch

terpene class of unsaturated isomeric hydrocarbons

contained chiefly in the essential oils of coniferous plants

timber wood suitable for building or structural purposes; growing or standing trees

tomentose covered with matted woolly hairs

topiary characterized by cutting or arraging shrubs, trees, etc. in fantastic or conventionalized shapes; ornamental gardens

transplantation to remove from one place and plant in another

tundra a rolling, treeless, often marshy plain of Siberia, Arctic North America, etc.

turpentine an oleoresin obtained from any of several coniferous trees, especially the longleaf pine, *P. palustris*

tussocks a tuft of hair or feathers

variety an individual or group of individuals that differ from the type of species in certain characteristics; a subdivision of a species

vasular consisting of ducts for transport of body fluids

vitriolic corrosive, burning or caustic

whorled a set of leaves, etc. on the same plane with one another, distributed in a circle

wood a hard fibrous material between the pith and the bark of a tree or shrub

xylem the portion of a vascular bundle in higher plants associated with the transport of water

zoologist a student of zoology, the science that treats of animals with reference to their structure and function

Index of English Names

Boldface numerals indicate illustrations.

General Index